Key H
for

Modern
America

Chris Macdonald
and
Jon Nichol

Stanley Thornes (Publishers) Ltd

For Joshua and Rebecca

Text © Chris Macdonald and Jon Nichol 1996

Designed and typeset by Hilary Norman
Illustrations by Peter Harper and John York (p. 41)
Picture research by Julia Hanson

Original line illustrations © Stanley Thornes (Publishers) Ltd
1996

First published in 1996 by:
Stanley Thornes (Publishers) Ltd
Ellenborough House
Wellington Street
CHELTENHAM GL50 1YW
England

96 97 98 99 00 / 10 9 8 7 6 5 4 3 2 1

A catalogue record for this book is available from the British
Library.

ISBN 0-7487-2597-0

Cover photograph: Rex Features

Printed and bound in Hong Kong

Acknowledgements

b = bottom, t top, l left, r right, c centre

Camera Press 67;

David Low/Evening Standard 'If we don't let him work,
who's going to keep him?'/The Centre for the Study of
Cartoons and Caricature/Solo Syndication 60;

Corbis UK Ltd 4, 10, 12, 14, 19t, 20, 21, 22, 23, 24,
26b, 27, 28, 30, 31c, 34t & b, 36, 38, 40, 42, 43, 44,
45, 46, 48, 49, 50, 51r, 52, 56l & r, 62, 64, 65, 66,
68, 69, 71, 72, 73, 74, 75, 78t & b, 80, 81t & b, 82,
83, 84, 85, 86r, 92–3;

Mary Evans Picture Library 71, 16;

John Frost Historical Newspapers 86l;

The Granger Collection 9, 13, 26t, 63;

Ronald Grant Archive 15;

Hulton/Reuters 88;

Imperial War Museum 7r, 11, 58;

Marilyn Silverstone/Magnum Photos 77t;

Peter Newark's Western Americana 17, 19b, 54, 59;

Popperfoto 77b;

Rex Features 70, 89, 90–1, 94, 95;

Spectrum Colour Library 8;

Topham Picturepoint 25, 53.

Every effort has been made to contact copyright
holders. The publishers apologise to anyone whose
rights have been overlooked, and will be happy to
rectify any errors or omissions.

Other Key History titles for GCSE:

Key Themes of the Twentieth Century (Philip Sauvain)
Russia and the USSR (Richard Radway)
South Africa in the Twentieth Century
(Hamish Macdonald and Barry Williamson)

A Teacher's Guide accompanies each title.

Contents

Introduction 4

America's government 5

1 America in 1919 6

Background: America and the First World
  War 6
America in 1919 8
Politics 10
Isolation 11

2 The Roaring Twenties 12

The Jazz Age 12
Hollywood 15
The economy – boom 18
The economy – the other side 20
Prohibition 22
Gangsters 24
The Ku Klux Klan 27
The American Government, 1920–29 30

**3 The Great Crash and Depression,
    1929–33** 32

Background 32
The Great Crash, 1929 34
The Depression 36

4 The New Deal 40

The 1932 presidential election 40
The New Deal, 1933–36 42
Farming, 1933–36 46
Opposition to the New Deal, 1935–36 50
The New Deal – success or failure? 54

**5 America and the Second World
    War** 58

The arsenal of democracy 58

6 Post-war America 60

The end of isolationism 60
The anti-Communist witch hunt,
  1946–54 64
America, 1945–60 68
President Kennedy, 1960–63 70
Death of a President 72
The Space Race 74
War on Poverty, 1963–68 75

7 Civil rights 76

The beginnings 76
The bus boycott 78
Schools and colleges 80
'I have a dream' – Martin Luther
  King 82
1990s race conflict 87

8 Political turmoil 90

America at war: Vietnam 90
Watergate 94

Index 96

Introduction

Look in the newspapers, listen to the radio or watch TV and you will always find stories about America. This is partly because the United States is still the richest and most powerful country in the world. It is also one of the biggest (Source **A**).

Exploring just one of the 50 states can take a long time. For instance, find the state of Texas on a map of the USA. The whole of England can be fitted into this state three times! There is a greater variety of landscape in the United States than in any other country in the world (Source **B**).

Modern America tells the story of the United States from 1918 to the 1980s. We want you to ask the same kind of questions as historians. For example, the picture in Source **C** is evidence about a famous event in American history.

- What is there to suggest that important people were travelling in the car?
- How can we tell that the car was accelerating when the picture was taken?
- What is there to suggest that the people shown in the photograph were completely surprised by what has just happened?
- Is there any evidence that the photographer was also unprepared for what happened?
- Is the photograph a primary or a secondary source?

The event that took place seconds before this photograph was taken horrified people around the world. The event was so important that historians believe 90 per cent of American adults knew about it within 30 minutes of it taking place. You can find out more about what happened on pages 72–73.

Source A By Alistair Cooke, an English-born reporter who became an American citizen

The first thing the foreigner has to take in about America is simply the size of the place, and the variety of life that goes on inside it.

Source B By Alistair Cooke

There is the east coast that goes from skiing country, through fertile farmland, to semi-tropical swamps and warm winter resorts. Westward over the Appalachian mountains and across the broadest stretch of land, a huge fertile prairie rising to the Great Plains. And on the west coast, from north to south there are virgin forests, falling away to the green, damp, England-like Oregon, down through all the various landscapes of California . . . to the desert and sun-soaked seashore of Lower California.

Source C A major event in America's history

America's government

How is America governed?

We live in a democracy. Can you say what the word means? Our closest ally is another democracy, the United States of America. How is the USA governed?

Source **A** should help you find out. America was run in the same way in 1918. Once you know how America's government works, you can make sense of the rest of this book.

Source A   American government now

One country – 50 states

In some ways the United States of America is not one country but 50: there are 50 states of the Union, each with its own government, courts, laws and police force. Every state has a **governor**. Within the states each of its towns and cities has a mayor who runs its affairs.

The United States is a **democracy**: more elections are held in America than in any other country in the world. There are elections for the US President, Senators, Congressmen, local politicians and mayors. In some states even judges and police chiefs are elected.

The Constitution

The most important rules of American government are laid down in the United States Constitution. The rules of the US Constitution are a check on the powers of Congress and the President.

The Supreme Court

The highest court in America is the Supreme Court. The Supreme Court has the power to declare a law 'unconstitutional' (against the Constitution).

Congress

Congress has to agree to all laws. Two houses make up the Congress: the **Senate** and the **House of Representatives** (a bit like the British House of Lords and House of Commons).

Congressman is the term for a member of the House of Representatives. Voters elect them for two years at a time. Voters elect **Senators** for six years. There are two Senators from each state.

The President

Elections for President are held every four years in November. The new President is sworn in the following January. A President can only serve two four-year terms in office. If a President dies or resigns, his Vice-President becomes President.

Political parties

There are two main political parties in the United States: the **Republicans** and the **Democrats**. To run for President a candidate has to be nominated by one of these two parties.

Election campaigns cost millions of dollars, so most of the candidates for President are very wealthy people.

The American People

1 Study Source **A** closely. Then try to answer these questions. What is:
  - the Supreme Court
  - the White House
  - the Senate
  - the House of Representatives?
  - Congress
  - the Constitution

2 Build up cuttings of information from newspapers and magazines on how America's government works. In groups, you can pool your cuttings. Organise them under the headings of the diagram.

Questions

1 America in 1919

Background: America and the First World War

Why did America enter the war?
What impact did the war have on America?

The First World War (1914–18), shaped America's history from 1919. In August 1914 the First World War broke out in Europe with Germany and Austria-Hungary against Russia, France and Britain. Like most Americans, America's ruler, President Woodrow Wilson, hated the idea of war. Wilson wanted America to stay out of the war and to concentrate on home affairs. However, the American government found it harder and harder to stay neutral.

America and Germany

As the war raged in Europe, most Americans began to turn against Germany. Why? Here are some facts to think about:

- On 7 May 1915 the British passenger liner *Lusitania* was sunk by a German U-boat – 128 Americans were among the passengers who drowned.
- In the same year German U-boats torpedoed several US merchant ships by mistake. Despite this swing in popular opinion, Wilson was re-elected in 1916 on a policy of keeping America out of the war.
- Germany seemed to back Mexico's plans to attack America. In January 1917, British agents produced evidence showing that the Germans were plotting to help Mexican rebels invade Texas, an American state.

On 2 February 1917, Woodrow Wilson cut off diplomatic relations with Germany, the first step to declaring war. In Source **A** an American reporter explains why.

Source A By an American reporter

On January 31st (1917) Germany announced that the following day a great war zone, surrounding Great Britain, France and Italy, and also in the Eastern Mediterranean, would be established and that 'All ships met within the zone will be sunk'. In the next two or three weeks at least two American ships were sunk . . . many other ships also with Americans on board. There is no question that Germany itself has been astonished that it has not long ago been at war with the United States.

War

On 2 April 1917, Woodrow Wilson made a speech to both Houses of Congress and asked them to declare war on Germany (Source **B**).

Source B By Woodrow Wilson, 2 April 1917. In the Library of Congress, Congressional Papers 1917

American ships have been sunk, American lives taken. We have seen the last of neutrality. We must fight for the peace of the world and for the liberation of its people, the German peoples included. The world must be made safe for Democracy. We are but one of the champions of mankind.

Booming America

The war in Europe led to a business boom in America. Private banks lent huge sums of money to the Allies at high rates of interest. Britain and France used this money to buy war materials from the United States. American industries expanded quickly, taking on more workers to provide war supplies. In 1915 about one in three of British shells fired in France had been made in the United States (Source **C**).

Source C From a report in *The Times* in 1916

One of the new factories has grown up on a spot which last November was green fields. Now there are 25 acres covered with buildings, packed with machinery. Most of the machines are of American make and some are marvels of modern design.

US big businessmen made huge profits. The workers profited, too: between 1914 and 1919 the average wage in America went up by 25 per cent.

From April 1917 American industries were brought under close government control for the first time. To pay for the war, government bonds were issued and taxes on the rich were increased. Those who opposed the war faced tough penalties. Under the Sedition Act of 1918 sentences of up to 20 years in prison could be imposed.

American troops

All men between the ages of 21 and 30 had to register for the armed forces (Source **D**). Soon over three million soldiers were being trained (Source **E**).

In March 1918 American troops tipped the balance of the war against Germany. The German war effort began to collapse. By the time the last guns stopped firing on 11 November 1918, 115,000 American soldiers, sailors and airmen had been killed.

Source E A patriotic poster calling Americans to arms

Source D An American recruitment poster for the First World War. What does the poster suggest about memories of the *Lusitania*?

1 Under the heading 'Wilson and the War', draw up a chart or information diagram or make brief notes on the following points:
- isolationism
- the business boom 1914–18
- the *Lusitania*
- Wilson's re-election in 1916
- America and Germany 1914–17
- the Mexican crisis
- America's entry into the war
- America's role in the war (Source **E**).

2 a) Draw up a list of the arguments that *either* a German immigrant in March 1917 might have made against America joining the war, *or* a British immigrant might have made in favour of joining.
b) Display your ideas in written or pictorial form.
c) As a class, hold a debate between the two groups: supporters of Germany, and backers of the Allies.

America in 1919

▶ **Was America a land of opportunity in 1919?**

A land of immigrants

Have you or your friends recently moved home? Why did your family move? What did they hope would be better? Before 1919, America was a new home to millions of new families. Do you recognise the first thing they saw when they approached New York (Sources **A** and **B**)?

Source B The words on the Statue of Liberty

Give me your tired, your poor,
Your huddled masses yearning to breathe free,
The wretched refuse [rubbish] of your teeming shore.
Send these the homeless, tempest-tossed to me.
I lift my lamp beside the golden door.

All Americans, apart from the native American people, once known as 'the Red Indians', are descended from people who have travelled to America as immigrants from other countries, or are immigrants themselves. By 1919 nearly 40 million people had emigrated to the United States, mainly from Europe. It was the biggest movement of people in recorded history. In 1919 over 14 per cent of people living in the United States were foreign-born and there were over 2,000 newspapers printed in languages other than English.

Most Americans believed that their country was the 'Land of the Free'. Unlike the countries of Eastern Europe, the United States was a democracy (see page 5). There was freedom of speech, a free press and freedom of religion. Compared with most countries America was a land of opportunity.

In 1919 people in the United States already had the highest standard of living in the world. How does Source **C** suggest this happened?

Source C The growing importance of the United States: US production figures and those of chief competitors in 1900

Source A The Statue of Liberty, New York

	USA	Main rival
Coal production (tons)	262 million	219 million (Britain)
Exports (£)	311 million	390 million (Britain)
Pig-iron (tons)	16 million	8 million (Britain)
Steel (tons)	13 million	6 million (Germany)
Railways (miles)	294,500	45,000 (Germany)
Silver (fine oz)	55 million	57 million (Mexico)
Gold (fine oz)	3.8 million	3.3 million (Australia)
Cotton (bales)	10.6 million	3 million (India)
Petroleum (metric tonnes)	9.5 million	11.5 million (Russia)
Wheat (bushels)	638 million	552 million (Russia)

From *History of the 20th Century*, Phoebus Publishing, 1976

Rich and poor

In 1919 the United States was a rapidly changing country. Americans were living in the richest country in the world, and in the world's greatest democracy. Yet money was still concentrated in the hands of a few people. Surveys showed that about 1 per cent of the people of America owned 50 per cent of the country's wealth, and the top 12 per cent owned 90 per cent of the wealth. The United States was a country of great opportunities for those in a position to take them.

The West

By 1919 a spider's web of over 320,000 miles of railroad covered the United States, more than in all of Europe. The railroads had changed the face of America. Every year hundreds of thousands of people migrated west by train. Most of the people migrating to the west at this time were looking for work in America's growing industries. But some were still going west to become 'homesteaders' and to claim land for themselves.

Towns and cities

Most Americans in 1919 lived in towns and cities. These were growing fast. In many there were huge, overcrowded, squalid slums (Source **D**).

Source D
A slum in New York's Lower East Side

Industry – 1919

About 70 per cent of American industrial workers worked over 10 hours a day. Some steelworkers faced a 12-hour day, seven days a week. Long hours and low wages led to bitter disputes. Huge firms or trusts ran much of America's economy.

Black Americans

Most American blacks were very poor. American blacks are the descendants of slaves. Slavery was only abolished in 1865, at the end of the American Civil War, when the northern states had invaded the Old South. In 1919, blacks were still second-class citizens and in the southern states many were little better than slaves. The south remained poor compared with the north.

1 a) How might you feel on first seeing the Statue of Liberty as an immigrant?
b) What does Source **B** tell you about the United States?
c) What does the number of foreign language newspapers in 1919 suggest about America?
d) What evidence is there in Source **C** that Americans were better off than other people?
e) What might it have been like to have lived in the slum in Source **D**?

2 If you had found yourself living in America in 1919:
• What hopes and fears might you have had?
• Where might you live?

• What job might you do?
• How might you become rich?

3 Use the evidence on these pages and anything else you can find out to write a letter home to your best friend as if you were an immigrant to America in 1919. In your letter, mention:
• arriving in New York
• living in a poor part of the city
• your decision to travel west
• what you saw on your journey.
Discuss these points with a partner before you write the letter.

Questions

Politics

▶ Was America a fair society in 1919?

Source A Woodrow Wilson (seated) with his chief adviser

In 1919 Woodrow Wilson had been America's President for seven years. A member of his government described him as 'clean, strong, high-minded and cold-blooded'. As President, Wilson was the most powerful man in America. What impression do you think he wants the photograph in Source **A** to give?

The world's greatest democracy?

In 1919 many Americans believed they were living in the world's greatest democracy. How democratic was it?

- First, in the southern states blacks were treated as second-class citizens. Any changes were hard to achieve, because the whites stopped them from having the vote. Pages 76–77 look at how whites denied black people their rights.
- Second, only four states permitted women to vote in elections. In America, as in Britain at this time, there was a growing campaign to win votes for women.
- Third, some of the most powerful people in America had not been elected at all. They were the owners of America's biggest companies, called trusts, such as the Standard Oil Company, the House of Morgan Bank, and the General Electric Company. Standard Oil was the biggest of all the companies (Source **B**).

Standard Oil has spared no expense in finding and making use of the cheapest methods of production. It has looked for the best workers and paid the best wages. It has invested millions . . .

Source B By John D. Rockefeller, owner of the Standard Oil Company

The trusts made millions of dollars' profit each year, but paid their workers badly. As a result, there were clashes between workers and employers. Between 1900 and 1919 there were more violent strikes and disputes in the United States than in any other country. Some companies even paid armed men to break up strikes and demonstrations. Men died in the fighting.

Questio

1 **a)** In what three ways was the United States not democratic in 1919?
   b) Why were industrial relations so bad in America?
   c) Refer to Source **B** to suggest why trusts like Standard Oil were so powerful.

2 If you had been an American citizen in 1919, what changes would you have liked to see in American society and in American government? Use the evidence on these pages and in Chapter 2 to make a list of reforms that you think were needed. How does your list differ from those of other members of the class? Try to persuade them round to your point of view.

Isolation

Why did America cut itself off from Europe?

The war to end all wars

Woodrow Wilson wanted to set up a strong international body, the League of Nations, to prevent war. At the Versailles peace conference in 1919 (Source **A**), the other Allied leaders were happy to set up the League. But when Wilson returned to the United States he found that most Americans were strongly against the Versailles Treaty. Under the Constitution the Senate has to ratify (agree to) all treaties with foreign countries. Why was opposition to the Versailles Settlement so strong?

Source A 'Versailles, 28 June 1919' – a painting by Sir William Orpen. How might enemies of the Versailles Settlement use this picture?

Opposition to the Versailles Settlement

Americans were against the Versailles Treaty for many different reasons:

1 There was a general feeling that the United States had been fighting someone else's war. Many Americans had lost friends and relatives in a war that was being fought over 3,000 miles away

2 Most German-Americans felt that Germany had been betrayed at Versailles.

3 Right-wing Republicans argued that Wilson had not been tough enough on Germany.

4 Left-wing Democrats said Wilson had been too tough on Germany.

5 Irish-Americans were also angry. Since 1916 the Sinn Fein Movement in Ireland had been fighting to win Irish independence from Britain. Irish-Americans said that

Wilson had done nothing at Versailles to see that the Irish people were treated fairly.

6 Some leading Senators and Congressmen disliked Wilson. They thought he was arrogant and a hypocrite.

7 Many Senators felt that the President was too powerful. They wanted the Senate to control foreign affairs.

8 Party politics: 1920 was a presidential election year. Republican leaders did not want the Democrats to be able to tell the American people that their party's government had not only won the War but also brought about a successful peace treaty.

9 American soldiers could be called upon to defend a country anywhere in the world. To millions of Americans, joining the League of Nations seemed to be like signing a blank cheque.

In March 1920 the Senate rejected the Versailles Treaty. Wilson was not a candidate in the 1920 election. The Republican candidate for President was Warren Harding. Harding backed the policy of isolationism: 'We seek no part in directing the destinies of the World.' Warren Harding won a landslide victory. And so the United States returned to a policy of isolationism.

Questions

1 Why did so many Americans oppose the Versailles Settlement?

2 Imagine you are an opponent of the Versailles Settlement. Design an election leaflet explaining why Americans should reject it.

2 The Roaring Twenties

The Jazz Age

▶ **What might it have been like to live in America in the 1920s?**
Why was Lindbergh an American hero?
How did life change for young women in the Twenties?

Have you heard of the Swinging Sixties? You can ask your mum, dad and grandparents about that time. How swinging were they really? The Roaring Twenties – the Jazz Age – was like the Sixties. The Twenties seemed to be a time of fun, with cocktails, a new dance (the Charleston), night clubs, cinemas, cars, singing and dancing, freedom and prosperity. Or was it?

If you had lived in America you may have been well off. The 1920s were boom years for the American economy. Between 1921 and 1929 wages rose from an average of $1,308 a year to $1,716. Despite this, many people still lived in poverty.

Entertainment

Young Americans wanted to forget about the war. They set out to enjoy themselves as never before. A whole pleasure industry grew up, giving Americans new entertainments to spend their money on. The 1920s were the heyday of silent movies. Screen stars like Charlie Chaplin, Buster Keaton, Laurel and Hardy became household names. Cinemas sprang up in every town and city. Hollywood, in California, became the centre of the film industry.

Source A By a jazz musician of the 1920s

Music is entering more and more into the daily lives of people. The negro musicians of America are playing a great part in this change . . . They have new ideas and constantly experiment. They are causing new blood to flow into the veins of music. The Jazz players make their instruments do entirely new things, things trained musicians are taught to avoid . . . Jazz has come to stay because it is an expression of the times . . . the breathless, energetic, super-active times in which we are living.

Source B A jazz concert in the 1950s. How might concerts like this appeal to young people in the 1920s, who had been 'brought up' on ballroom dancing?

Spectator sports

The 1920s were also golden years for spectator sports such as baseball, basketball, boxing and American football. Radio broadcasts, newspapers and magazines helped to turn sports stars into national heroes.

Source C A report from the *New York Times*

A flashing, red-haired youngster, running and dodging with the speed of a deer, gave 67,000 spectators jammed into the new $1,700,000 Illinois Memorial Stadium the thrill of their lives today. Illinois smashed Michigan 39–14 in what will probably be the outstanding game of the 1924 season in the West.

Harold (Red) Grange . . . doubled and re-doubled his football glory in the most incredible show of running, dodging and passing seen on any ground in years. A show that set the spectators screaming with excitement.

Heroes – Charles Lindbergh

One of the most famous American heroes from the Jazz Age was Charles A. Lindbergh. On 20–21 May 1927 he became the first man to fly solo across the Atlantic in his plane, 'The Spirit of St Louis' (Sources **D** and **E**).

Source D   Report in the *New York Times*, 11 June 1927, on the return of Charles Lindbergh to America

This is a big thing Lindbergh has done. We shouted ourselves hoarse. Not because a man has flown the Atlantic! Not even because he was an American! But because he is clear in character as he is strong and fine in body, because he put what he believes in before any desire for wealth, because he is modest and courageous and these are the things we most honour in life.

Source F   From the *New York Times*, 11 June 1927

His reception in both Washington and New York was an incredible triumph. His ship arrived on 10 June. America's first greeting to the great flier was given a hundred miles out at sea by four destroyers. The ship was escorted in by the four ships and forty aeroplanes.

New York gave Lindbergh a hero's ticker-tape welcome. Mountains of torn-up shreds of paper poured down from the buildings and covered the streets as he passed.

Women in the twenties

Life also changed for American women. During the Great War millions of women had taken over jobs that only men had done before. Women proved that they could do any job just as well as men. The money the women earned gave them a new freedom. In the 1920 presidential election, women were able to vote for the first time. Some young women, who called themselves 'flappers', made a point of showing they were free to behave as they liked (Source **G**).

Source E   Charles Lindbergh and his plane 'The Spirit of St Louis'. How does the plane give us some idea of Lindbergh's achievement?

Source G   What one flapper wrote in the *New York Times* in 1922

Of course a flapper is proud of her nerve . . . She is shameless, selfish and honest but at the same time she thinks of these things as good. Why not? She takes a man's point of view as her mother never could. When she loses she is not afraid to admit defeat, whether it be a lover or $20 at an auction.

She can take a man – the man of the hour – at his face value, with no foolish promises that will later be broken. She will never make you a hatband or knit you a necktie, but she'll drive you from the station on hot summer nights in her own sportscar. She'll put on trousers and go skiing with you or if it happens to be summer time, go swimming. She'll dive as well as you, perhaps better. She'll dance as long as you care to and she'll take everything you say the way you mean it, not getting sore or hurt . . .

More women worked and invested money on the stock exchange (Source **H**).

An age of extremes

'Crazes' and 'fads' were common in the Jazz Age – pastimes such as the Chinese game Mah Jong, or going to dance marathons. The Charleston dance was 'all the rage'. Perhaps the craziest fad was flagpole sitting (Source **I**)! The record was set at 23 days and 7 hours.

Source I Champion flagpole sitter Alvin 'Shipwreck' Kelly

Source H From the *New American Review*, April 1929

There is a surge of women investors: secretaries, heiresses, business women and housewives. In the last ten years the number of women speculators has increased from 2 per cent to 35 per cent of the huge army that daily gambles on the stock market.

The best-selling writer F. Scott Fitzgerald was writing in the 1920s (Source **J**).

Source J From F. Scott Fitzgerald, *Echoes of the Jazz Age*, 1931

The parties were bigger, the pace was faster, the shows were broader, the buildings were higher, the morals were looser and the liquor was cheaper.

The dark side

There was another, darker side to the Jazz Age. It was a time of gangsters and illegal alcohol (see pages 22–26). It was also an age of incredible prejudice. In the case of the Ku Klux Klan (see pages 27–29), this prejudice brought terror to millions of people and cost many their lives.

Questions

1 **a)** How did jazz change things (Sources **A** and **B**)?
   b) Why did American football have a wide appeal (Source **C**)?
   c) Why was Lindbergh a hero (Source **D**)?
   d) What in Source **G** suggests that flappers were rich girls?
   e) Why might Kelly have sat on his flagpole (Source **I**)?

2 Produce a 'Roaring Twenties' scrapbook, explaining:
   • what things happened and why
   • what life was like for young people.
   Use the headings in this unit to help you.

Hollywood

What was the appeal and impact of Hollywood?
What does Charlie Chaplin's career tell us about America in the 1920s?

Hollywood's impact

During the next week, keep a record of the number of TV programmes and films you see that were made in Hollywood, California. By the early 1920s, Hollywood had become the film capital of the world. Over 90 per cent of films shown in British cinemas were American.

Early films

These early films were 'silent movies'. From the 1920s thousands of would-be film stars moved to California in the hope of getting into the movie business. Most never made it. Soon Hollywood studios were competing with each other to produce the most expensive and star-studded feature films. One of the most famous of these was *Beyond the Rocks*, which was made in 1922 (Source **B**).

Source A By Joseph Kennedy, 1927

The motion picture industry has achieved a standing and a size that makes it impossible for people studying industry to overlook it. It is already the fourth largest industry in the country. Yet it is an industry that has developed only in the last ten or twelve years.

Source B From Gloria Swanson, *Swanson on Swanson*, 1980 – Gloria Swanson's autobiography

Everyone wanted *Beyond the Rocks* to be every exciting thing Hollywood could serve up in a single picture. It would have the glamour of Swanson, the Latin magic of Rudolph Valentino and would be a wonderful love story. In the story I played a poor but noble English girl who is married off to an elderly millionaire, only to meet the love of her life on her honeymoon. There were historical flashbacks so that Rudy and I could wear costumes of some of the most romantic periods of European history. The wardrobe department made me a gold-beaded evening gown so beautiful that movie-goers talked about it for the next year. I also wore over a million dollars worth of jewels.

Source C Gloria Swanson in one of her elaborate costumes

RUDOLPH VALENTINO

236.P.
LES' POSTCARDS

The stars

Hollywood stars found that there was a price to pay for fame. Reporters wanted to know every detail of their private lives. Gloria Swanson suggested that the public expected very high standards from the stars they worshipped (Source **E**).

Source E From Gloria Swanson, *Swanson on Swanson*, 1980

At the age of 25 I was the most popular female star in the world except possibly for my friend Mary Pickford. I was also the first star in the pictures to be marrying a European with a title. All over the world fans were rejoicing because Cinderella had married the prince. What the press and fans did not know was that I was pregnant. I knew that if they found out my career would be finished. The industry and the public would reject me as a morally unsound person unfit to represent them.

The American film industry

- People like Gloria Swanson, Charlie Chaplin, Buster Keaton, Rudolph Valentino and Mary Pickford became stars of the silent screen.
- Cinemas hired piano players to provide background music during the films.
- In 1927 an average of 60 million people went to the cinema each week in the United States.
- In 1928 the first 'talkies' were made.
- 110 million went to the cinema each week in 1929.
- Hollywood studios made over 500 films a year.
- In the 1930s Hollywood stars found that they were also having to compete with cartoon characters! Walt Disney turned Mickey Mouse, Pluto, Goofy and Donald Duck into household names.
- In the 1950s television began to challenge the cinema.

Scandal!

By 1922 many of the top men in the movie business feared that the mounting number of Hollywood scandals would in the end ruin the whole motion-picture industry. So the leading studios set up a censorship office. One of the first rules was that kisses should run for no longer than ten feet of film. So each kiss scene was shot twice, once for the version to be released in America and once for the European version. In her autobiography *Swanson on Swanson* (1980), Gloria Swanson describes her early days as a film actress (Source **F**).

The American movie industry only began to decline with the coming of television after the Second World War.

I worked with an English comedian. His name was Charlie Chaplin and he was the highest paid actor on the pay-roll . . . Everyone said he was very funny with his little moustache and seedy clothes. When he came to the Essanay [the studios] the management let him try out anyone he might like for a comic partner. He picked me and spent one whole morning trying to get me to work up routines with him. These all involved kicking each other in the pants, running into things and falling over each other. He kept laughing and making his eyes twinkle and talking in a light and gentle voice and encouraging me to let myself go and be silly.

Source G Charlie Chaplin in one of his film roles. Why was he dressed in this way?

This is the great picture upon which the famous comedian has worked a whole year.

6 reels of Joy.

Charles Chaplin IN "THE KID"

Charlie Chaplin

Source **G** shows Chaplin at work. He became one of the greatest comedians in history and people flocked to see him in films such as *Dough and Dynamite*, *The Vagabond*, *The Pawnshop* and *The Gold Rush*. His later films included *Modern Times* (1936) and *The Great Dictator* (1942). Chaplin and several other leading movie stars decided to start their own film company. They called it 'United Artists'.

Like many of the early Hollywood stars, Charlie Chaplin came from a very ordinary home. Chaplin's story and those of other Hollywood stars encouraged people to believe in the 'American Dream', that anyone can make it in America if they have talent and work hard enough.

Charles Chaplin

Charlie was born in 1889 in London. His family were so poor they had to enter a workhouse to get food and shelter to live. He first went on stage when he was five years old. In 1910 he emigrated to the United States. In 1915 he started his famous film character 'Charlie' with the toothbrush moustache, bowler hat and clumsy walk.

In 1918 at the age of 29 he married the 16-year-old actress Mildred Harris. They were divorced in 1920. When he was 35 he married 16-year-old Lolita McMurry but this marriage did not last either.

He spoke out against the dropping of two atomic bombs on Japan in 1945. He was accused of being pro-communist and anti-American. So he left the United States to live in Switzerland.

Questions

1 **a)** What does Source **B** tell us about the kinds of films Hollywood was making in the 1920s?
   b) If you had the chance, would you go to see films like *Beyond the Rocks*? Why do you think people went to see these films?
   c) Think of as many words and phrases as you can to describe Gloria Swanson (Source **C**).
   d) On average, how many people went to the cinema each week in the United States in 1927? Why do you think this figure had risen so much by 1929?
   e) How important was the film industry, and what impact did it have on people's lives? Interview some people you know who are over 60 about the role the cinema played in their lives when they were your age.

2 **a)** What image of Gloria Swanson did her studio try to give in publicity photographs like the one in Source **C**?
   b) According to Gloria Swanson in Source **E**, what were the top men in the movie business worried about? Why?
   c) What is there in Source **E** to suggest that the public had a very romantic view of Hollywood stars?

3 **a)** What can we learn about Gloria Swanson from Sources **C**, **E** and **F**?
   b) What can we learn about Charlie Chaplin from Sources **F** and **G** and the text?
   c) Sources **B**, **E** and **F** are taken from Gloria Swanson's autobiography *Swanson on Swanson*, which she completed in 1980. Do you suspect that anything she says in these extracts may be untrue? Why?
   d) Suggest two reasons why autobiographies are sometimes unreliable as sources of evidence.

The economy – boom

How and why did American industry boom in the 1920s?

The economy

Many American industries boomed in the 1920s. The economy doubled in size. Mass-produced consumer goods poured from the production lines of electrified factories. America soon left the age of the horse behind. Henry Ford led the way in mass-producing goods (Source **A**).

Source A From *America* by Alistair Cooke, 1973

Ford made his radical breakthrough by thinking first of the needs of hundreds of thousands of consumers . . . In 1914 the national average wage was $2.40 a day. Ford paid a minimum of $5.00. His first touring Model T cost $850. By 1926, when he had quadrupled the average wage to nearly $10, the Model T sold for only $350 and had a self-starter . . .

Beginning in the early 1920s, people who had never taken a holiday beyond the nearest lake or mountain could now explore the South, New England, even the West, and in time the whole horizon of the United States. Most of all, the Model T gave to the farmer and rancher, miles from anywhere, a new pair of legs.

Henry Ford

Businessmen such as Henry Ford worked hard to find out how to make things more quickly and cheaply than before. Ford invented an 'assembly line' to produce his Model T Ford motor cars. How did the system work? The workers stayed in one place while the motor car moved past them (Source **B**).

Source B Description of a car assembly line, by Henry Ford

Electricity

- The use of electric power increased the speed and efficiency of industry.
- In 1914 electricity only powered 30 per cent of factories. This had risen to 70 per cent by 1929.
- From 1921 the number of fridges soared from 5,000 to 900,000 and radios from 50,000 to 10 million.

The car

- In 1920 there were eight million cars in America. During the 1920s over one million Model T Fords were produced each year.
- Two other huge car firms, Chrysler and General Motors, boomed in the 1920s.
- By 1930 America had enough cars – about 23 million – to squeeze every American into one.
- By 1930 businessmen such as Henry Ford had turned the automobile (motor car) business into America's most important industry.
- The car industry contributed 13 per cent to US manufacturing production. The jobs of over four million people depended on it.

Impact of the car

- The car had a huge impact on American life, roads, suburbs, garages, petrol stations, hotels and restaurants.

In the chassis assembly line there are 45 separate operations . . . some men do only two small operations, others do more. The man who places the part does not fasten it. The man who puts the bolt in does not put the nut on, the man who puts the nut on does not tighten it . . . On operation No. 34 the motor gets its petrol . . . on operation No. 44 the radiator is filled with water, and on operation No. 45 the car drives onto the road.

Source C Part of the Ford assembly line. What might it have been like working on this assembly line eight hours a day?

All the Model T Fords, nicknamed 'Tin Lizzies', were painted black, as this helped to keep down costs.

The electric age

The 1920s were also the electric age. Using mail catalogues, you could buy thousands of goods (Source **D**). Sewing machines, vacuum cleaners, washing machines, typewriters and cookers were also mass-produced on assembly lines. A whole new advertising industry grew up to sell these new products. This in turn helped other industries to expand.

Source D A page from a mail-order catalogue

Hire purchase

Advertising encouraged people to buy goods even if they did not have the money. People could obtain things on credit, through hire-purchase (HP) and other schemes.

The building trade

The building trade boomed as well. 'Sky-scrapers' completely changed the skyline of many American cities. New York's Empire State Building, built in the 1920s, was the tallest building in the world.

Source E
From a newspaper report

From the feeble wireless telegraph service in 1920, radio has grown in ten swift years into the billion-dollar industry it is today. Advertising has made broadcasting an industry. The broadcasters discovered they could boost the car industry or the ginger beer industry. And then time on the air becomes something that people want to buy. Television is just around the corner. In another ten years will it be in our homes?

Questions

1 **a)** Why and how did the following industries change in the 1920s:
   - film
   - car
   - electrical
   - advertising
   - mail order
   - broadcasting?

   b) Why was an assembly line the most efficient way of making cars (Source **B**)?

2 How might the growth of industry in the 1920s have changed people's lives? Think of someone working in a large city: life at home (kitchen, living room, bedroom), buying things, where people lived, travel, working in a Ford car factory, holidays, buildings, entertainment.

The economy – the other side

Why were many Americans badly off in the 1920s?

Not everyone did well during the boom years of the Jazz Age in the United States. The boom's main impact was in the industrial northern states.

- In 1929 the average wage in the north-east was $881 a year (£196). In the south-east it was $365 (£81) a year.
- Millions of Americans continued to live in poverty. A survey showed that six out of ten Americans did not have enough money to buy sufficient food or to pay for adequate housing.
- Wealth was shared out very unevenly.

Problems

- The government had not fixed a minimum wage.
- Trade unions were weak.
- There was no state health system, no state pensions, no unemployment pay and no sickness pay.
- Trusts and cartels could fix prices so that they were high.

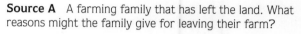

Source A   A farming family that has left the land. What reasons might the family give for leaving their farm?

Farming

Farming slumped as European farming recovered after the First World War and Europe no longer needed as much American meat and grain. American farmers also increasingly had to compete with farmers in Argentina and Canada.

- President Coolidge vetoed (turned down) Bills passed through Congress that were aimed at guaranteeing farm prices.
- Many smaller farmers went bankrupt.
- During the 1920s, six million people left the countryside to live in the cities (Source **A**).
- By 1930 over half of American people were living in the 100 biggest cities.

Industry

In industry, too, there were problems. In 1918 and 1920 there were major strikes in the coal and steel industries against low pay and dangerous working conditions.

- Coal mining was depressed because of competition from new sources of power – hydro-electricity, natural gas, oil.
- The coal miners' strike in West Virginia only ended when the Governor called in state troopers to smash it.
- President Harding set up an inquiry into conditions in the mines. Its findings largely supported the miners. But the government took no action.

Strikes in the textile industry

Some of the worst disputes were in the textile industry. The cotton textile industry was depressed. Artificial fibres were replacing cotton. In Asia new factories were making goods more cheaply than in America.

- Textile workers knew they risked everything if they went on strike, because the textile companies usually owned the homes of the workers.

- In 1927 the United Textile Workers Union went on strike in Elizabethtown, Tennessee. Here girls were working 56 hours a week for 18 cents an hour. The strike ended when police and state troopers arrested pickets (Source **B**).

- Further strikes followed in North Carolina and Virginia. Again force was used to break the strikes.

Source B
A striker being arrested. How would the factory owners justify the action of the police?

Government and workers

- In almost every major strike action of the 1920s, the government backed the management against the workers.

- The Supreme Court also declared that two state laws banning child labour were 'unconstitutional'.

- It also banned laws setting a minimum wage for women workers.

- Many people left the unions when strike action failed to lead to better working conditions and pay.

- In 1920, 5.1 million Americans were members of unions.

- In 1929, 3.6 million people were union members.

1 **a)** What do Sources **A** and **B** tell us about life for some Americans in the 1920s?
   b) What problems faced the coal, steel, textile and farming industries in the 1920s?
   c) Why were textile workers risking everything when they went on strike in 1927?
   d) Why did membership of trade unions decline in the 1920s?
   e) Why did government do little to protect farmers and industrial workers?

2 Produce a report that lists:
   a) the problems facing the American economy in the 1920s
   b) suggestions for making life better for the worst-off in America.

Questions

Prohibition

Why did Prohibition occur?
What were the consequences of Prohibition?

Drinking banned!

How do you think people would feel if the government banned the sale of alcohol and told pub owners that they could only sell soft drinks from now on? In January 1918, the 18th Amendment to the United States Constitution was passed that did just that.

The Volstead Act backed up the 18th Amendment, saying that 'liquor' was any drink that contained 0.5 per cent alcohol or more (beer is usually at least 5 per cent alcohol).

The Prohibition campaign

The Women's Christian Temperance Union and the Anti-Saloon League had long campaigned for Prohibition. They believed that the only way to end the evils of drunkenness and alcoholism was to ban (prohibit) the sale of drink. Their campaign had massive support from the deeply Christian American people. They argued that drink was a waste of grain for food, it caused a drop in output from farms and factories, and led to death on the roads.

Enforcing Prohibition

The new law came into effect at midnight on 16 January 1920. America went 'dry' – no alcohol was to be made, transported or sold. This was easier said than done (Sources **A** and **B**).

Smuggling alcohol into the United States from Mexico and Canada became big business.

Bootleggers

People who made or smuggled illegal liquor were known as bootleggers. (The name was first used in the seventeenth century, when the British still ruled the thirteen states. Smugglers would hide liquor in their high leather boots to avoid the British taxes.) Illegal drinking saloons – speakeasies (Source **C**) – sprang up in nearly every town and city in the United States. They were called 'speakeasies' because customers had to speak quietly so that they were not discovered. Before Prohibition there were about 15,000 legal

Source A   Beer kegs were smashed, and the beer flowed in the streets

Source B   A reporter in 1930 describes an attempt to round up stills used to make alcohol in New York

The Administrator had 178 agents to search [for stills] among 1,278,431 homes . . . It was almost impossible to find the sources of liquor when they were hidden away in city homes or, in the case of the big producers, when it was hidden away in some hollow or wood. Often they were so out of the way that even the owner of the land did not know about it. For instance, a large still producing 130 gallons was found going at full blast in Texas on the farm of Senator Morris Sheppard. Sheppard had been the proposer of the 18th Amendment.

saloons in New York. By 1932 there were about 32,000 speakeasies in the city.

Source C
A speakeasy.
What might it
have been like
to visit this
speakeasy?

The Prohibition Agents were not just 'kill-joys'. Moonshine (illegally-brewed) liquor could be dangerous, even fatal. Another terrible result of Prohibition was gangsterism (see pages 24–26).

In 1933 the Prohibition Amendment was repealed. After signing it Roosevelt said: 'I think this would be a good time for a beer'.

The statistics in Source **D** show how drunkenness seems to have increased in Philadelphia during the Prohibition period.

Source D Arrests for drinking offences in Philadelphia 1920–25

Year	Drunks	Disorderly conduct	Drivers	Alcoholics	Total
1920	14,313	6,097	–	33	20,443
1921	21,850	5,232	494	33	27,609
1922	36,299	7,925	472	50	44,746
1923	45,226	8,076	645	177	54,124
1924	47,805	6,404	683	874	55,766
1925	51,361	5,522	820	814	58,517

Figures from the Philadelphia Police Department

In order to deal with the speakeasies, 1,500 Prohibition Agents were appointed. One of the most famous of these agents was Izzy Einstein (Source **E**).

Source E From a report in the *New York Times*

In rum-running circles the name of Izzy Einstein has become a curse among rum-drinking people . . . [he] decided that the way to catch the rum sellers was to look and dress and act the part of people of all classes and walks of life except the unwelcome one . . .

Questions

1 **a)** What arguments were there in favour of Prohibition?
b) Why did it have popular backing?
c) What did Prohibition mean (Source **B**)?
d) What do Sources **C**, **D** and **E** tell us about the effectiveness of the Prohibition Law?
e) Why might Source **D** be unreliable as a source of evidence about breaches of Prohibition in Philadelphia?

2 Copy and fill in the table below, showing the main events during the era of Prohibition.

Topic	Notes
January 1918	
Prohibition	
Volstead Act	
Support	
1920	
Enforcement	
Distilling	
Smuggling	
Speakeasies	
Prohibition Agents	
Moonshine	
Gangsters	

3 **a)** If you were asked to stamp out cigarette smoking in your school, how would you go about it? Draw up a plan of the action you would take. How successful do you think it would be? What problems might you face?
b) What does this tell you about the problems faced by the enforcers of Prohibition?

Gangsters

▶ Who were the gangsters?
Why did they flourish?
What part did they play in American life?

Every city had its gangsters. In New York, Dutch Schultz held sway, Chester La Mare ran Detroit, and Dion O'Banion was king of Chicago. Dion was a jolly man, full of jokes, who sang in the choir of the Holy Name Cathedral. The headquarters of his gang was his

Source A Dion O'Banion, described in 1981 in an interview with Jack McPhail, who was a Chicago crime reporter in the 1920s

Source B Al Capone. What messages do Capone's looks, clothes and body language send about him?

flower shop. Yet O'Banion murdered at least 25 people. He led the Irish-American gangsters of Chicago and like many others he made himself rich through bootlegging liquor. O'Banion's gang controlled most of the bootleg business in south Chicago.

▶ Several of his famous murders were due to his sense of humour. He would tell one gangster: 'Joe he's saying the most dreadful things about you, you've ever heard!' Then there'd be a shoot-out between the two of them. O'Banion made fun out of dying.'

Torrio

Another gangster, John Torrio, ran an Italian-American gang who were members of the Mafia. Soon Torrio and his gang controlled the whole liquor trade in North Chicago.

- O'Banion and Torrio bought up most of the old breweries and distilleries in Chicago and began producing liquor on a large scale.
- Torrio started up thousands of speakeasies.
- He brought in truckloads of Canadian liquor every night.
- Torrio hired a young gangster, Al Capone, soon to be the most famous mobster of them all (Source **B**).

Al Capone	
1899	Alfonso Capone was born in New York, the son of Italian parents who had emigrated to America.
1918	He fled from New York after beating a policeman to death with his pistol.
1920	John Torrio hired Capone to help him run his empire.
1927	Capone helped to get the mayor of Chicago, the gangsters' backer, re-elected.
1929	Capone murdered his main rivals in Chicago.
1931	He was arrested and charged with not paying his taxes. He was sentenced to eleven years in prison.

Political corruption

The Mayor of Chicago was Big Bill Thompson. Torrio soon gained control over him by offering him huge bribes.

- Big Bill did not interfere in the gangsters' activities.
- Thompson sacked city officials who caused problems for Torrio.
- Many of the badly-paid police force were also ready to accept bribes.
- In 1923 Bill Thompson was defeated in the election for mayor.

The new mayor was honest. He planned to deal with the gangsters and with bootlegging. Torrio and Capone decided it was time to move their base to a safer place away from the centre of Chicago, to the town of Cicero.

Control over Cicero

The gangsters picked Cicero, a wealthy, middle-class suburb of Chicago. To make Cicero safe for themselves they decided to take control of the town council. They put up their own candidates in the 1924 election (Source **C**).

Source C A newspaper report describes how the gangsters got people to vote for their candidates

Cicero – election day

Automobiles filled with gunmen paraded the streets slugging and kidnapping election workers. Armed thugs raided polling places and even forced voters to vote for Torrio's candidates.

- The Cicero voters appealed to the Chicago police department for help.
- Seventy policemen rushed out to Cicero.
- There was a pitched battle in which some gangsters, including Capone's brother Frank, died.
- But Capone's candidates were elected and Cicero was brought under the mob's control.

Gang warfare

The rival gangs of Chicago fought each other there and in other cities for control of the liquor trade. The Thompson sub-machine gun became their favourite weapon. They fondly called it the 'typewriter' because it could fire 1,000 rounds a minute. It could also cut through quarter-inch-thick steel when fired at close range.

Capone was strong enough to move against his rivals. His gangsters walked into Dion O'Banion's shop and sprayed him with machine-gun bullets. To show that there were no hard feelings, Capone sent $50,000 of flowers to the funeral in 26 lorries. O'Banion's coffin itself cost $10,000 (Source **D**).

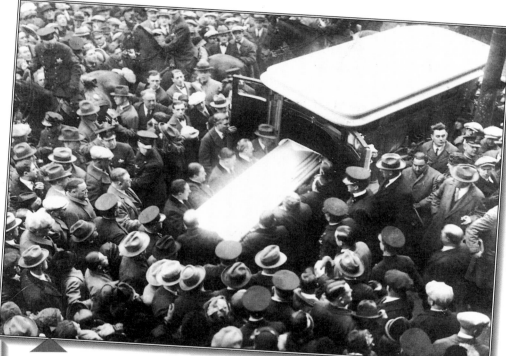

Source D O'Banion's funeral procession. What idea does the photograph give of O'Banion's importance?

Capone in charge

O'Banion's murder led to a series of revenge gangster killings. In one attack John Torrio was badly wounded. Capone escaped unhurt although his car was riddled with bullets. Torrio decided to retire from gangster life. Capone now took complete control of Torrio's empire, with an income of about $100 million a year. No one is sure just how rich he was as he kept his money in cash. Capone had made himself the most powerful man in the state of Illinois. Bodyguards followed Capone everywhere. Capone's V8 Cadillac car weighed over seven tons, had armour plating and bullet-proof windows. At the back it was fitted with machine-gun mountings (Source **E**).

Yet Capone claimed he was just another businessman (Source **F**).

Source E Capone's car. Why did Capone need a car like this? What impression does it give?

Source F By Al Capone, 'just another businessman'

If people didn't want beer and wouldn't drink it, a fellow would be crazy going around trying to sell it. I've seen gambling houses too in my travels and I never saw anyone point a gun at a man and make him go in. I never heard of anyone being forced to go to a place and have some fun . . .

I help the public. You can't cure thirst by law. They call me a bootlegger. Yes. It's bootleg while its on the trucks, but when your host hands it to you on a silver plate it's hospitality.

1929: Capone triumphs

The gangster wars reached their height in 1929. Bugs Moran, who had taken over O'Banion's old gang, killed a friend of Capone's. Source **G** shows how Capone took his revenge. Seven leading members of Bugs Moran's gang were mown down in their meeting place in North Clark Street in the St Valentine's Massacre on 14 February. Moran himself arrived at the meeting late and decided that it was a good time to take a walk. He escaped getting murdered by a few minutes. No-one was ever charged with the crime. Between 1927 and 1931 there were 227 gang murders in Chicago. No one was ever convicted.

Source G The St Valentine's Day 'massacre'. What might the photographer have thought and felt when he took this picture?

Questions

1 a) What do we learn about Dion O'Banion from Sources **A** and **D**?
   b) Who was Big Bill Thompson?
   c) Why were the Chicago police easy to bribe?
   d) How did Capone and Torrio take over Cicero? Why?
   e) What happened to Dion O'Banion? Why?

2 a) Can we rely on Sources **B**, **F** and **G** as sources about Capone ? Why/Why not?

   b) What do we learn about Al Capone from Sources **B**, **E**, **F**, **G** and the text?

3 Design the front page of a Chicago newspaper for 15 February 1929 (the day after the St Valentine's Massacre). Include details of: the massacre; gang rivalry in Chicago; Capone's career; funerals. Also include a cartoon or picture, and an editorial (column where the paper gives its views) on how the gangsters can be brought to justice.

The Ku Klux Klan

What was the Ku Klux Klan?
How strong was it in the 1920s?
Why did it decline?

Study Source **A**. Source **B** contains clues about what is happening in Source **A**.

Source A A Ku Klux Klan initiation ceremony. What do you think the scene shows? Who are the people in the picture?

People watching a night parade of robed Klansmen marching in fours were at once silenced by the ghostly scene. The column extended in the glare of one street lamp after another, as far as the eye could see. The white-robed figures were covered with pointed hoods. Their bodies were draped in loose white cassocks [a kind of robe]. The dead whiteness of the uniforms was matched with the dead silence of the marchers. There were many flaming crosses and American shields. Amongst most of the marchers there was not an eye or a face or a hand in sight.

Source B From a magazine report

The Ku Klux Klan stirred up hatred and prejudice against blacks, Jews and Catholics (Source **C**). Klan members swore an oath of loyalty to America, and to fight 'any cause, government, people, sect or ruler that is foreign to the USA'.

The Klu Klux Klan

- Southern whites founded the Klan after the American Civil War.
- The Klan beat up and killed thousands of blacks in the South.
- In 1919 all the states of the Old South brought in 'Jim Crow laws' which said that blacks should be 'separate but equal'.
- Blacks and whites were kept apart in every public place, including trains, schools, prisons and restaurants.

- During the First World War many thousands of blacks moved to the northern cities to do the new jobs that the war created.
- At the end of 1921 the Klan's leader, William Simmons, claimed that the Klan had 100,000 members.
- By 1924 the leader Hiram Evans claimed the Klan had a membership of nearly five million.

Source C A Klan hanging. How might one of the people who is watching describe what is happening?

Blacks in northern cities

As the blacks usually ended up doing the worst jobs, most white people did not really mind at first. However, the movement to the cities led to housing shortages. In 1918 and 1920 there were riots in many northern towns. The worst riots were in Chicago. Thirty-three people died in the first week. Many homes were burned.

Ku Klux Klan in the 1920s

The Ku Klux Klan used the riots to stir up racial hatred. Its membership began to grow. One magazine drew up a report on the Klan's activities (Source **D**).

Source D
From the New York *World* magazine

Our reporters have discovered:

  5 kidnappings
43 orders to negroes to leave town
27 tar and featherings
41 floggings
  1 branding with acid
  1 mutilation
  4 murders

In 1923 Hiram Wesley Evans became the Klan's leader, or 'Imperial Wizard'. Support for the Klan was spreading across America. Outside the southern states the Klan was more anti-Catholic than anti-black (Source **E**).

In many ways the beliefs of the Ku Klux Klan were like those of the Nazis in Germany and the Fascists in Italy (Source **F**).

Source F   By Hiram Wesley Evans

The Klan was much stronger in the countryside than in the towns (Source **G**).

Source G   From a magazine published in 1928

Hundreds of people in the larger cities had no contact with the Klan. They felt that the whole movement could be laughed out of existence. Few ever gave that view after seeing a robed Klan review.

The decline of the Ku Klux Klan

In Indiana the Ku Klux Klan was so strong that its chief, D. C. Stephenson, said, 'I am the law in Indiana'. Stephenson called himself the 'Grandest Dragon of the Empire'. Through bribes and blackmail he came to control many of the state's politicians.

- In 1928 Stephenson decided to run as a candidate for the US Senate. He said that his aim was one day to become President.
- However, Stephenson became involved in a kidnap case. He was accused of abducting a girl and frightening and abusing her so much that she took poison. Even then, he refused to get help but left her to die.
- Stephenson was found guilty. Instead of going to the Senate, he was sent to jail for life.
- Stephenson's action stunned America. It even shocked most Klansmen, and millions left the movement.

Millions of Americans stood up to the Ku Klux Klan and spoke out against its ideas and actions. All over America clergymen, teachers, reporters and many others were prepared to condemn the Klan. After this the movement collapsed, but it did not die out altogether. Even today some Americans belong to the Ku Klux Klan.

Source E   From a magazine report on a meeting in Indiana

Crosses were burnt near Catholic churches or on hill tops. A cross was built of timber and covered in kerosene and then set on fire. These crosses flashing through dark nights drove many a good citizen to his home.

There are three great racial instincts which must be used to build a great America: loyalty to the white race, to the traditions of America and to the spirit of Protestantism . . . The pioneer stock must be kept pure. The white race must be supreme not only in America but in the whole world . . . The world had been so made that each race must fight for its life, must conquer or accept slavery or die.

The Klan believes the Negroes are a special problem. The Klan wants every state to bring in laws making sex between a white and black person a crime. Protestants must be supreme. Rome shall not rule America. The Roman Catholic Church is un-American and usually anti-American.

Questions

1 **a)** Write brief notes on the following:
- origins of the Ku Klux Klan
- William Simmons
- Jim Crow laws
- Klan beliefs, supporters, organisation and activities
- collapse of the Klan.

b) Why do you think the writer of Source **B** described the scene as 'ghostly'?

c) What is going on in Sources **A** and **C**? What can we learn about the Ku Klux Klan from such photographs?

d) Study Source **C** carefully. Why might someone wish to take such a photograph?

e) Why did the Klan light fiery crosses (Source **E**)?

f) What clues does Source **F** give us about why the Klan hated Catholics?

g) The Klan declined after Stephenson was charged with murder. Does this suggest that most Klansmen did not fully support their leaders' ideas? If so, why?

2 Imagine that you are investigating the activities of the Ku Klux Klan for a magazine. You have all of the sources and the text to help you.
- Use all the evidence you can find to reconstruct what is going on in Sources **A** and **C**.
- What might people in the pictures have told you?

The American Government, 1920–29

How well was America ruled in the 1920s?
Why did America clamp down on immigration?
What was the Red Scare?

The Republican decade

From 1921 to 1929, America's Presidents were Republicans. President Warren Harding (1921–23) wanted to remove all the special powers that the government had gained between 1914 and 1918 in the First World War. One of Harding's first acts as President was to remove all the war taxes on the rich, and government controls over business.

Corruption

Harding was a cheerful rogue who liked pretty girls and parties.
- He gave key posts to corrupt friends from his home state of Ohio.
- Harding's government soon became one of the most corrupt in American history.
- The most famous scandal was over an oil deal, the Teapot Dome affair (Source **A**).
- Harding died in Alaska in August 1923.

Calvin Coolidge

Harding's Vice-President, Calvin Coolidge (1923–29), was sworn in as the new President in an emergency ceremony which took place in a Vermont farmhouse by the light of a kerosene lamp.

Coolidge achieved little as President, although he introduced tax cuts for the rich. Between 1924 and 1928 taxes on incomes of over a million dollars a year were reduced from $600,000 to $200,000. When Coolidge died, Dorothy Parker's remark, 'How could they tell?' echoed what many people actually thought.

America and the rest of the world

During the 1920s, America's relations with most European countries were poor. Wilson's policy of encouraging free trade was scrapped.

In 1922 the Fordney-McCumber Tariff Act placed high tariffs (duties) on all foreign-made goods sold in the United States, so that American goods were cheaper. European countries then placed tariffs on American-made goods. A trade war broke out.

Source A The Teapot Dome scandal. In 1922 the US Secretary of State for the Interior, Albert T. Hall, was accused of accepting huge bribes in return for cheap leases to oil companies on the Teapot Dome oilfields in Wyoming. The President declared: 'If Hall is not honest, then I'm not fit to be President.' Hall was later charged, found guilty and sent to prison.

During the First World War the United States had lent its allies over $10.25 billion. The British Government suggested that the United States should cancel some of these debts to help Europe recover from the war. President Coolidge (1923–29) simply replied: 'They hired the money, didn't they!'

Treaties to preserve peace

In 1922 Warren Harding got the Senate to agree to the Washington Treaty by which the United States, the major countries of Western Europe, and Japan promised to limit the size of their navies.

The United States followed the treaty and scrapped fifteen warships. Japan ignored the treaty and during the 1930s launched a big shipbuilding programme. By 1941 Japan's navy was stronger than the British and American Pacific fleets together.

The Kellogg-Briand Pact

In 1928 the US Secretary of State, Frank Kellogg, along with the representatives of 61 other countries, signed the Pact of Paris, to preserve world peace.

Immigration

After the First World War, immigrants flooded into America. The government decided to put a stop to this.

- The Immigration Act of 1921 limited the number of immigrants allowed each year from Europe, Australia, the Near East and Africa to 3 per cent of the numbers of their nationality who were already living in the United States.
- In 1929 immigration was cut to only 150,000 a year (Source **B**).

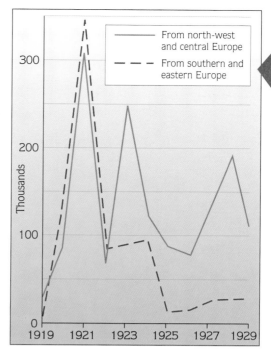

Source B Immigration into the USA, 1919–29

The Red Scare

By 1919 Russia had fallen to the Bolsheviks. Germany was on the brink of revolution. Many Americans feared communism would spread to America.

- In 1919 a bomb blew out the front of the house of America's Attorney-General. A man died. The government blamed Communists for the bomb.
- In May 1920, the police arrested two Italian immigrants, Sacco and Vanzetti, for taking part in a wages robbery. They were anarchists who wanted an end to government. Anarchists used bombs and guns.
- Sacco and Vanzetti had loaded guns. One of these guns fired the same kind of bullets as those used in the raid. Witnesses said they had carried out the raid and that they were anarchists.
- Other witnesses said they were elsewhere when the raid took place.
- The two men spoke no English.
- The case against them was weak. Even so, the jury found them guilty. The judge sentenced them to the electric chair. Later he said to a reporter: 'Did you see what I did to those anarchist bastards!'

Despite nationwide protests (Source **C**), Sacco and Vanzetti were executed seven years later. Many 'Reds' were immigrants and were deported. By the late 1920s the Red Scare seemed to be over.

Source C Demonstration against the execution of Sacco and Vanzetti, April 1927. Which organisations are supporting Sacco and Vanzetti?

Questions

1 How well do you think America was ruled in the 1920s?

2 How well did America get on with the rest of the world in the 1920s?

3 Why did America clamp down on immigration?

4 What was the Red Scare?

5 Do you think Sacco and Vanzetti were guilty or innocent?

3 The Great Crash and Depression, 1929–33

Background

 What led to the Crash?

In October 1929 the American stock market crashed – the price of shares dropped like a stone. Why did this matter? The stock market raised money for the American economy, for example for the building and running of factories and mines, the buying of ships, trains and lorries for trade, the buying of raw materials. Cut off the cash and business stops. So millions of Americans lost their jobs as thousands of firms went bust and farmers left their farms. What lay behind the Great Crash?

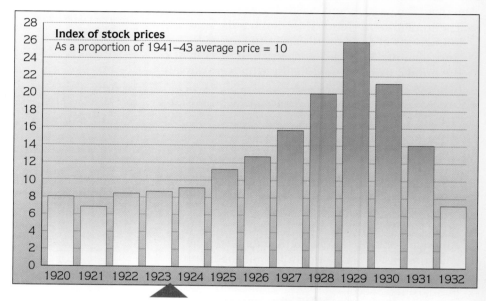

Source A   The value of shares, 1920–32

Gambling on the Stock Exchange

In the 1920s people began to gamble on the Stock Exchange in a way they had never done before.
- Share prices went up and up.
- This in turn meant that the demand for shares increased. People saw the chance to make easy money simply by buying shares. You could buy shares and sell them later, keeping the profit.
- You might even borrow money to buy shares, knowing that you could pay back your loan later.
- So the prices continued to rise.
- As long as shares were in demand their prices would go up.
- Source **A** shows how the value of shares rose in the 1920s.

Something for nothing!

Many people could see no reason why share prices should not continue going up for years. Clearly many shareholders had little idea about what they were doing. During the 1920s the buying and selling of shares seemed an easy way for hundreds of thousands of Americans to make money (Source **B**).

Source B   Written by a businessman in 1928

The numbers of inexperienced speculators [people who gamble on the stock market] are being increased by a great many men who have been attracted by newspaper stories. These stories tell of the big, easy profits to be made on the Stock Exchange and of millions of dollars being made by some people overnight. At first these newcomers risked a few hundred dollars with some broker they knew. They discovered that it could be easy to make money in this way. Finally they would bring with them their entire savings accounts.

These amateurs have not learnt that markets sometimes panic and there are large falls in prices. These suckers speculate on tips, on hunches, on 'follow-the-leader principles'. When a company rises quickly on the Stock Exchange they all jump for it. They buy or sell at the slightest notice.

Newspapers told their readers how to make quick profits for no work (Source **C**).

Source C
The front page of the *New York Times*, 15 July 1928

The New York Times.

Section 9 — SPECIAL FEATURES AUTOMOBILES

SPECIAL FEATURES RADIO—AVIATION — Section 9

SUNDAY, JULY 15, 1928.

NATION-WIDE FEVER OF STOCK SPECULATION

Eager Buying Has Reached All Classes of People Throughout the Country and Has Set New Records In Many Directions—Effects of Struggle to Grasp Profits in Trading in Securities Are Evident

America was booming. Most American companies had been doing well (see pages 18–19).

Problems facing the US economy before the Wall Street Crash

1 Many shareholders were using borrowed money to buy shares. People were even buying shares on hire purchase. You only had to put down 10 per cent of the purchase price to buy a share. Between 1927 and 1929 American stockbrokers increased the amounts they had borrowed from $3.5 billion to $8.5 billion. This meant that share buyers were forcing up share prices with money they did not really have. The American economy was becoming a bit like a balloon. Once pricked, it would collapse.

2 Many big American companies were facing problems of making too many goods. This overproduction meant they were making goods that people could not buy, even on credit. In 1927 the spending power of American people per head began to fall.

3 Some major industries such as farming, textiles and coal had been depressed all through the boom years.

4 United States trade with other countries was going down. Ever since the Fordney-McCumber Tariffs (see page 30) had been introduced, other countries had been putting high tariffs (taxes) on American goods being sold in their countries. This meant that American companies were failing to sell to foreign countries the extra goods they were producing.

- As they grew they took on more workers, producing more goods.
- People who bought shares in companies that were doing well were paid good dividends as the companies made big profits.
- This meant that more and more people wanted to buy shares.

Firms made big profits and could pay out more money each year (dividends) to their shareholders.

In fact, as some experts realised, the American economy had big problems (see box on left). Things were fine so long as share prices rose. But what if they fell?

Questions

Write a radio broadcast entitled 'The Causes of the Wall Street Crash of 1929'. It should be about 500 words long, and should contain interviews and eyewitness reports.

a) It should deal with the long-term causes of the Crash. Consider the following:
- gambling on the stock market
- the role of the papers in pushing stock market fever
- the rising price of shares
- profits in industry
- why the economy was like a balloon
- over-production
- the weakness of farming, textiles and coal
- trading difficulties

b) Put these causes into what you think are their order of importance.

The Great Crash, 1929

What was it like to live through the Great Crash in October 1929?

An Italian immigrant, Luigi Barzini, remembers the Crash well. He was at college, and his teacher had asked the class to imagine they were working for a newspaper. Their task was to design the front page based on that day's stories (Source **B**).

Source A A victim of the Wall Street Crash. Wall Street, New York, is where brokers bought and sold shares for people on the stock market. Why is this man selling his car?

Source B Luigi Barzini, *O America: A Memoir of the 1920s*, 1977

It was Thursday 24 October 1929, the day the dam burst on the American economy. It was a frantic day. There were two very big news stories to worry about. An anarchist had tried to kill the Italian Prince Umberto in Brussels. And the price of shares had collapsed on Wall Street. Thousands of people seemed to be ruined. Which story should take up the main column of the front page?

The assassination story looked much more interesting. After all, Americans are so interested in any thing to do with royalty. . . On the other hand the Wall Street story did not look nearly so attractive. The Exchange had had a few slumps in the past and a few serious ones in previous days . . . Some of the country's most important bankers and political leaders told the people that they should not panic . . .

I wrote 'Wall Street' at the top of the front page in the layout in bold letters.

Pictures like the one in Source **C** were to be seen in the newspapers that week.

Source C Investors rush to Wall Street as news of the Crash spreads

Losing money on Wall Street

Share prices had to keep rising so that people who had bought shares with borrowed money could pay for them later. Should share prices fall, how could you pay for the shares you had already bought? And if you and others were forced to sell, the share price would fall again.

- More sales would mean lower share prices.
- Banks would demand to have back the money they had lent you.
- Lower share prices would force more sales to pay for debts.
- More sales would mean lower share prices.
- Lower share prices would mean . . .

and so on, and so on. We call this a 'vicious circle'.

The Crash

So what happened in the Crash? The main events were these:

September/October 1929 Many professional share dealers guessed that the stock market could not rise for ever. Some rich shareholders began to sell shares, thinking prices were at their peak. Prices stopped rising.

19 October Many dealers got nervous. More traders started to sell large blocks of shares.

21 October Prices began to fall sharply.

24 October The Wall Street Crash began. Sales became a flood. Panic had set in. On the 'day the dam burst', over 12 million shares changed hands. Efforts to stop the collapse in prices failed.

Monday 28 October The New York Times Average Share Index fell by 43 points. It was the biggest one-day fall in US history. Thousands of owners of shares rushed to sell them. Share prices fell like a stone.

29 October The US stock market collapsed completely. 16 million shares were traded. As hardly anyone wanted to buy shares, most of these were sold for very low prices. Some people sold almost all their possessions to raise some money.

November 1929 Prices kept on falling. Hundreds of thousands of Americans stared ruin in the face (Source **D**).

Source D
Luigi Barzini remembers

Famous firms went bankrupt. Brokers jumped to their deaths from the top of skyscrapers. The price of shares sank ever lower after brief rallies . . . People I knew were down and out. Some put up their houses for sale, a useless act as no one was buying anything, or boarded them up and left because they could no longer afford to live there . . . An old couple who lived not far from us lost everything in the Crash. It was too late for them to start life again so they committed suicide.

Questions

1 Like Luigi Barzini, you have been asked to design a front page for a newspaper based on the main news stories for 29 October 1929. Include the following:
   a) Headlines, stories and pictures.
   b) An interview with Luigi.
   c) An interview with the man in Source **A**, on 19 October, 24 October and 29 October.
   d) A story saying:
   - what the Crash meant for people who had spent their life savings on stocks and shares, and who had borrowed money to buy them (Source **D**)
   - how important the Crash seemed at the time.

2 You can play a game as if you were 'playing' the American stock market in the 1920s. You have borrowed $1,000. You decide to spend it on shares in the companies listed in the table below. You have to put down 10 per cent of the share price only for each share bought.

Company	Share prices	Round 1 shares cost	Round 2 shares cost	Round 3 shares cost
American Canadian	$70			
Anaconda Copper	$50			
Electric Bond and Share	$90			
General Electric	$130			
United States Steel	$140			

Round 1
- Make out a table like the one above.
- Decide how many shares you will buy.
- Put the number bought and the total money spent in the 'Round 1' column.

Round 2
- Throw a dice. The numbers 1–5 show how much the share has *increased* in value: 1 = 10%, 2 = 20%, 3 = 30%, 4 = 40%, 5 = 50%. If you throw a 6, share prices stay the same. You can either *sell* or *buy* shares at these prices, using the money you have.
- Enter the correct figures in the 'Round 2' column.

Round 3
- The same rules apply for throwing numbers 1–5. If you throw a 6, share prices fall by 10% in this round.

Round 4
- For this and each following round, share prices *fall* by: 1 = 10%, 2 = 20%, 3 = 30%, 4 = 40%, 5 = 50%.

The Depression

 What impact did the Depression have on America?
What happened to the unemployed without homes or money?

Source A Unemployed men queue for bread and soup in New York. What might the men in the queue tell you has happened to them?

Source B By an unemployed worker in New York

I had tramped the sidewalks [pavements] for three days. Finally I stood in the breadline. To my surprise I found all types of people – the majority being skilled craftsmen – unable to find work. One had been a civil engineer and had earned $8,000 a year.

Source C Alistair Cooke, *America*, 1973. At the time of the Depression, Alistair Cooke, a young Englishman, had just arrived in the United States.

Only the very poor had nothing to lose. When steel stocks went from 90 down to 12, the automobile companies simply let half their workers go. There were skyscrapers just finished that had no tenants. There were truckers with nothing to truck, crops that went unharvested, milk that went undelivered to people who couldn't afford it. When I first arrived here, as a student in a college town, I couldn't go out in the evening to mail a letter without being stopped by nicely dressed men who had told their wives they were out looking for night work. So they were – they were out on the streets cadging dimes and quarters.

Source D By the historian Henry Steele Commager

As unemployment reached staggering levels the suffering became intense. Of New England's (North-Eastern states) 280,000 textile mill hands, 120,000 had no work a year after the Crash. In a country of 120 million people, probably more than 40 million were either unemployed or members of a family in which the main breadwinner was out of work. Those who did have jobs often worked for a pittance [a tiny amount]. Women in Tennessee textile mills got $2.29 for a 50-hour week . . . Grown men worked for five cents an hour in sawmills, Negroes learned the cruel truth of the saying that they were 'the last to be hired and the first to be fired'. Yet . . . orchards were heavy with fruit, granaries bulging with grain, factories loaded with clothing, Pennsylvania coal miners froze in the midst of mountains of coal while their children lived on weeds and dandelions.

Source E From Luigi Barzini, *O America: A Memoir of the 1920s*, 1977

Shops sold their stock at clearance sales and closed for ever. Unemployed men began selling apples or pencils in the street. They pretended that they were not simply begging.

I never thought that the Depression would last more than a few months and I never thought that it would spread to the whole world.

Source G From H. Brogan, *The Penguin History of the United States*, 1985

Farm incomes (which had benefited little from the boom) had fallen by more than half. But precisely because prices were so low, it would pay nobody to shift harvests to market. In Oregon sheep were slaughtered and left to the buzzards because farmers could afford neither to feed them nor to ship them. Wheat in Montana was left to rot in the fields.

Source F The American economy's vicious downward spiral

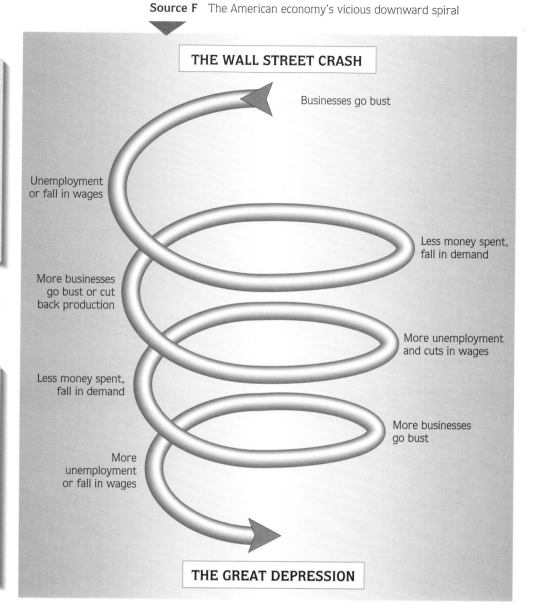

THE WALL STREET CRASH

Businesses go bust

Unemployment or fall in wages

Less money spent, fall in demand

More businesses go bust or cut back production

More unemployment and cuts in wages

Less money spent, fall in demand

More businesses go bust

More unemployment or fall in wages

THE GREAT DEPRESSION

The Depression, 1929–39

Banking
Between 1929 and 1932 over 5,000 banks went bust.

Trade
The value of America's foreign trade dropped from $9 billion to $3 billion.

Unemployment
Unemployment grew rapidly (Source **H**). By 1932 unemployment had risen to at least 12 million as more and more businesses went bankrupt.

Poverty
Breadlines like the one in Source **A** became a common sight all over America.

Farming
Farmers suffered greatly during the Great Depression. Thousands of families who had farmed their land for generations were forced to sell their farms. Millions of farm workers went to live in the big cities, hunting for work.

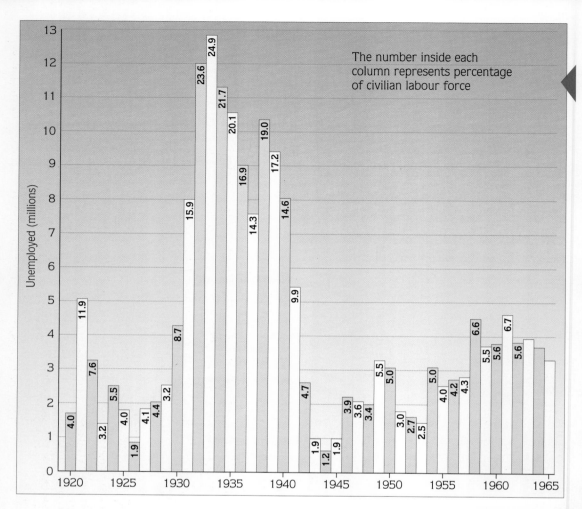

The number inside each column represents percentage of civilian labour force

Source H Unemployment in the USA, 1920-65. What does the graph tell you about the growth and extent of unemployment?

From Daniel Snowman, *USA: The Twenties to Vietnam*, Batsford 1968, revised edition *America Since 1920*, Heinemann Educational Books 1978

The impact of the Depression

Many unemployed people built themselves shacks on wasteground. These hovels made up townships, called 'Hoovervilles' after President Hoover (Sources **I**, **J** and **K**).

Source J By Arthur Schlesin

Source I A Hooverville. What might it be like to spend a day living in a place like this?

The cold was bitter in unheated tenements, in the flophouses [doss houses] smelling of sweat, in the parks, the empty freight [cargo] cars, along the windy waterfronts. With no money left for rent, unemployed men and their families began to build shacks where they could find land that was not already occupied. Along the railroad embankment, beside the garbage burner, in the city dumps, there appeared towns of tar-paper and tin, old packaging boxes and old car bodies. These communities were symbols of the Depression and were known as 'Hoovervilles' (after President Hoover). In many cases it was only the lucky ones who could find Hoovervilles. The unlucky ones spent their nights huddled together in doorways, in empty packing cases and in box cars. At the bread lines and soup kitchens, hours of waiting would produce a bowl of mush, often without milk and sugar, and a tin cup of coffee.

Prepare a talk entitled 'What impact did the Depression have on America?' to give to the rest of your class. To help you, work on the sources and the special boxes in this section, making notes on the following topics.
- The extent and growth of unemployment.
- The impact on textile (cotton factory) workers.
- The coal industry.
- Farming: sheep, wheat.
- Drift to the cities.

- Treatment of black people.
- Breadlines.
- Suffering caused by the Depression.
- Income.
- Food.
- Housing.
- Charity.
- Death.

Questions

Source K A description of a Hooverville in Chicago, from *Government and the Depression, 1929–32*

Last summer in the hot weather when the smell was sickening and the flies were thick there were hundreds of people coming to one of the dumps, falling on the heap of refuse as soon as the truck had pulled out, digging into it with sticks and hands. They would eat all the pulp that was left on the old slices of watermelon and they would take away and wash and cook turnips, onions and potatoes that had been thrown away.

Source L By Alden P. Hatch

Hoover had little to do with the financial disaster. The worst that can be said of him is that he did nothing. On the other hand, when he continued to do nothing in the face of such a tide of misery, that became a serious charge.

Source M By R. B. Nye

Hoover did a good job in fighting the Depression, but what he did was far from enough. Hoover urged 'Business as usual' and waited for the Depression to wear itself out.

Source N By Andrew Sinclair

Hoover's measures to cope with the Depression were too little, too late. Any Democratic candidate would have beaten Herbert Hoover in 1932.

Local government and charity

Local governments and private charities found it impossible to cope with the numbers of unemployed. In Cleveland, Ohio, unemployment reached 50 per cent in 1932. In June 1932 Philadelphia City Council ran out of money and stopped giving aid to 50,000 families. Many workers, faced with starvation, applied for government begging licences. The veteran soldiers of the First World War were bitter. All that they had fought for seemed to have fallen apart.

President Hoover and government action

President Hoover believed that it was up to private businesses to get America out of the Depression. He thought that government action in itself could do very little to reduce unemployment. To protect US industries against competition from foreign imports, he backed the Hawley-Smoot Tariffs in 1930. This simply made European countries increase their own tariffs on imported goods from America.

- In 1931 Hoover set up the Reconstruction Finance Corporation to help banks and finance companies that were in danger of going bust.
- He also increased spending on federal (government) building projects which created some new jobs.
- The Federal Farm Board bought large amounts of wheat and cotton to try to help farmers, but it did not buy enough, and farm prices continued to fall.
- Small-scale government projects started to give work to the unemployed, but they were on far too small a scale.
- President Hoover refused to start unemployment benefit.

There were widespread protest marches. The police often broke these up.

Sources **L**, **M** and **N** give three historians' views of Hoover.

Questions

Produce a collage for a wall display on 'The Depression' to show what people thought, felt and did at that time. Work on your own or in pairs or small groups.

1 Using the sources and text to help you, make working notes on the following.
   a) An unemployed person waiting in a breadline (Sources **A**, **B** and **J**).
   b) The growth and extent of unemployment (Sources **B**, **C**, **E**, **F** and **H**).
   c) A bankrupt farmer; moving to the town; life in a Hooverville (Sources **I**, **J**, **K**).
   d) Hoover's policies and their impact.
   e) Make a sketch of Source **I**. Use evidence from Sources **J** and **K** to annotate your sketch about the scene and the people in it.
   f) How reliable are Sources **J** and **K** as evidence about poverty in America?
   g) What evidence is there in Sources **L–N** that many people blamed President Hoover for their suffering?
   h) Do Sources **L–N** tell us anything about how historians think?

2 Prepare the collage.
   a) It needs a title, to be planned out under headings and to look good.
   b) You can include eyewitness accounts, interviews, extracts from original sources.
   c) Hold a classroom exhibition of your collages. Each person or group should talk about their own collages. Take a class vote on which one is the best.

4 The New Deal

The 1932 presidential election

▶ **How did Roosevelt win the 1932 election?**
How well would you cope with the problems of beating a depression like the one that hit America in the 1930s?

Hoover faced defeat in the 1932 presidential election (Source **B**).

Source B By Roosevelt's biographer, Alden P. Hatch, in *Franklin D. Roosevelt*

Hoover showed little patience with those out of work. Although he was prepared to help starving animals, he refused to support starving Americans. Typical was his treatment of the Bonus Marchers in June 1932. These veterans of the First World War had come to Washington with their families to demand from the government the bonus it had promised to pay them. Instead of giving them help Hoover sent armed troops in tanks to use tear-gas against the Bonus Marchers. The troops tore down the Bonus Marchers' Hooverville near to the White House and drove the marchers out of Washington.

Millions of our citizens cherish the hope that their old standards of living and thought have not gone forever. Those millions cannot and shall not hope in vain. I pledge you, I pledge myself to a New Deal for the American people.

Hoover's democratic opponent was Franklin D. Roosevelt, 'FDR'. FDR promised:
● to distribute food and money to all those on the breadline
● government plans to solve the crisis in banking, industry, trade and farming
● to set up large-scale government industrial projects to create new jobs.
Roosevelt offered hope to millions of hungry Americans. He promised to give the American people a 'New Deal' (Source **C**).

In September 1932 Roosevelt went on a 'whistle-stop' tour of the United States by train (Sources **D** and **E**).

Source E Some words from Roosevelt

Source C From Roosevelt's speech to the Democratic Party, 193

Source D Alden P. Hatch, *Franklin D. Roosevelt*

They waited for him in stadiums, at fair grounds and on little station platforms . . . Roosevelt made about 20 speeches a day and gained a thousand friends every 24 hours. Each time the train stopped, be it only by a water tank in the desert, he did up his braces and went out on the rear platform for a word and a joke with the cheering little crowd.

Every man has a right to life and this means that he has a right to earn a comfortable living. Every man has a right to his own property, which means a right to be sure that his savings are safe.

1 Joe and Jane Brown

They are cotton growers and live in the cotton bowl of Oklahoma. They are half starving and dressed in rags. Their soil is exhausted. Money from the sale of cotton is not enough to pay the mortgage to the bank.

5 Michael and Virginia Morgan

They are a very rich family who have made a fortune from making radios. They believe that the government can do nothing to stop poverty. The way for the country to recover is to let the market take care of itself.

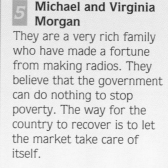

2 Alex and Mary Stedding

They were wheat farmers and have been forced to sell their farm. They have trekked to California along Highway 66.

6 Jerry and Maureen Swaggart

This family of teetotal Baptist preachers believe that drink is the source of all evil. They have worked hard to help the poor whom the Depression has thrown out of work.

3 Jim and Susan Weiskopf

Jim was a businessman who lost his fortune in the Wall Street Crash (see pages 34–35). He has had to sell his home and now he and his wife live in a Hooverville.

7 Mark and Mavis Jones

Mark is a veteran soldier from the First World War. He has spent a lot of time out of work. He and Mavis run a small café and work very long hours for little reward. The Depression has meant that there has been a fall in their income.

4 Kim and Louisa Ridoli

They are a gangster family from Chicago. During the '20s they made a fortune from selling illegal liquor. His mob openly bribe the police and local politicians.

8 Jim and Alice Smith

Jim runs a factory making woollen jumpers. He and his workers have had to take a cut in income and wages because they cannot sell their jumpers at a decent price. It is likely that with falling demand their factory will close.

Questions

1 a) List the problems that faced America in 1931.

b) Imagine you are one of Roosevelt's advisers. Write a draft manifesto (called a 'platform' in America) or a speech for Roosevelt for the 1932 election. In it outline the policies he should use in his campaign, and describe how he should attack Hoover. Think about:
- getting people back to work
- helping banks
- farmers and industry
- dealing with areas with high unemployment
- the problem of foreign trade
- providing help for the sick
- the Bonus Marchers.

How might you use photographs in your manifesto?

2 Which of the families 1–8 above do you think would support Roosevelt's election campaign, and which would oppose him? Say why.

41

The New Deal, 1933–36

> **What was the 'New Deal'?**
> **How did it try to solve the economic problems of America?**
> **Did the New Deal get America back to work? If so, how?**

Roosevelt as President

On 4 March 1933, Franklin Roosevelt was sworn in. In his first speech as President he pointed to the huge problems facing America (Source **A**).

Source A From Roosevelt's first speech as President

The immediate crisis: the banking problem

The day before the swearing-in ceremony, two more major banks had stopped trading. Experts feared that millions of people would rush to withdraw their savings, causing other banks to go bust. America faced a new economic crisis. The public were rushing to take their savings out of the banks (Source **B**). The banks would be forced to shut. Can you think why? This would mean no money for anything. How would people be paid, loans given to keep businesses going, money raised for new projects? Roosevelt at once called a Bank Holiday. The banks would close until a plan had been worked out to protect them.

This is above all the time to speak the truth, the whole truth, frankly and boldly. This great nation will revive and prosper. So first of all let me assert [state] my firm belief that the only thing we have to fear is fear itself . . .

Taxes have risen, our ability to pay has failed, government of all kinds is faced by serious cuts of income. The withered leaves of industrial enterprise [business] lie on every side. Farmers find no market for their produce. The savings of many years in thousands of families are gone. More important, many unemployed citizens face the grim problem of existence. An equally great number toil with little in return. Only a fool will deny the dark realities of the moment . . . This country asks for action and action now!

Source B A crowd desperate to get its money out of a bank. What rumours might be flying around in the crowd?

Source C From Alistair Cooke, *America* 1973

It was the day the money stopped; literally, you had to cadge a meal, live on the tab in places that knew you, pay with a cheque for a cab ride and once – I remember – for a shoeshine.

The New Deal: Relief, Recovery, and Reform

President Roosevelt used the slogan 'Relief, Recovery, and Reform' to describe how he would beat the Depression.

- **Relief** Roosevelt had to tackle the huge linked problems of poverty and unemployment.
- **Recovery** America had to get its unemployed back to work. All areas of American life needed a boost to stop factories, mines, trucks, trains and farms from standing idle.
- **Reform** Americans must never let the Depression happen again. This would mean changing the way they ran America.

In the next 100-day session of Congress, it passed laws faster than at any other time in American history.

Pages 43–45 look at the impact that these and other measures had. In 1934 Congress set up the Securities and Exchange Commission (1934) to end gambling in stocks and shares.

Industry and welfare

What did Roosevelt do to try to solve the problems of America's millions of unemployed workers? FDR had four main plans.

The Civil Conservation Corps

The Civil Conservation Corps, or CCC, was Roosevelt's own brainwave. He put young people to work to help conserve the countryside. Out-of-work, single young men were given six months' work. They lived in work camps on schemes such as digging ditches, building dams and planting trees to stop soil erosion. Soon the CCC found work for over 300,000 unemployed people (Source **D**).

The New Deal – 100 days of action

5 March President Roosevelt called Congress into special session.

9 March After debating for only seven hours, Congress passed FDR's Banking Act, giving the President new powers to control banking activities.

12 March Roosevelt made a nationwide radio broadcast urging people not to take their money out of the banks.
- This was the first of many radio 'fireside chats' over the next twelve years in which he told Americans what the government was doing.
- When the banks opened, more people put money in than took it out. The banking crisis was over and Roosevelt's New Deal had begun.

1. **Emergency Banking Act** – made sure that banks were soundly financed with government backing for their funds. It stopped the use of a bank's money for gambling on the Stock Exchange.

2. **Home Owners Loan Corporation** – provided new loans for home buyers. Over 300,000 loans were made within a year.

3. **Federal Emergency Relief Administration (FERA)** – gave money to states to help them provide better relief for the poor. It was headed by Harry Hopkins.

4. **National Industrial Recovery Act (NIRA)** – banned child labour and set up a maximum 36-hour week for industrial workers and 40-hour week for clerical workers. The Act also set up the Public Works Administration (PWA) to provide employment in the building of bridges, schools, hospitals, etc.

5. **Agricultural Adjustment Administration (AAA)** – gave money (subsidies) to farmers in return for cutting output.

6. **Farm Credit Administration (FCA)** – provided new loans to farmers at low rates of interest.

Source D Men at work. Who are they? What do you think they are doing, and why?

Federal Emergency Relief Administration

Roosevelt chose Harry Hopkins to head the Federal Emergency Relief Administration, or FERA. Harry Hopkins was a close friend of Roosevelt. What did the FERA do?

- **Money** The FERA handed out money for food, clothes, housing, tools, seed and livestock to the poor and needy.
- **Work** Hopkins got Roosevelt to agree to spend huge sums of money on public works schemes like airports and road building to get the unemployed back to work. Hopkins set up the Civil Works Administration (CWA) to spend the cash for relief (Source **F**).

Source F From Jon Nichol, *Work Out Modern World History*, 1990

Industrialists agreed to allow workers to form trade unions in return for the government ending laws against industries fixing their prices. Each industry agreed to work with the National Recovery Administration to agree an industry code to fix the hours of work, wages and conditions for men, women and children. The eight-hour day and agreed minimum wages became general. Codes were agreed for hundreds of industries, including the key ones of car manufacture, cotton, steel and coal. Child labour ended in coal-mines and cotton-factories and even Henry Ford, hater of trade unions, agreed to follow the code for the car industry. Firms which agreed to a code were allowed to use the symbol of the NRA, a blue eagle.

The FERA's work carried on through the mid-1930s. It built some 32,000 kilometres of sewers, 40,000 schools, 40,000 playgrounds and built or improved 1,000 airports, 400,000 kilometres of road and gave 50,000 teachers jobs.

Source E A description of the CWA, from R. E. Sherwood, *Roosevelt and Hopkins*, 1948

The CWA put four million people to work in the first thirty days of its existence and, in less than four months, inaugurated 180,000 works projects and spent over $933 millions. [Roosevelt was given a report on its progress from a friend, Frank Walker.] 'I saw old friends of mine – men I had been to school with – digging ditches and laying sewer pipes. They were wearing their regular business suits as they worked because they couldn't afford overalls and rubber boots.' One of them pulled some silver coins out of his pocket and showed them to Walker. 'Do you know, Frank', he said, 'This is the first money I've had in a year and a half? Up to now, I've had nothing but tickets that you exchange for groceries.'

Source G The NRA symbol. What ideas do you think the designer of this logo was trying to get across?

National Recovery Administration

The National Industrial Recovery Act set up the National Recovery Administration – the NRA. The NRA tackled two problems: how to get people back to work, and how to stop civil war breaking out between workers and their employers. The NIRA set up the Public Works Administration (PWA) which ran schemes along the same lines as the CWA and CCC. For example, the PWA built large housing projects, schools, hospitals and dams.

The Works Relief Bill (1935) set up a single body to run relief projects. The single body had two branches, the PWA and the WPA.

- **Public Works Administration (PWA)** – this ran large-scale projects like building dams, bridges and highways.

- **Works Progress Administration (WPA)** – under Hopkins it handled small-scale projects. It also found work for musicians and artists, doctors and teachers.

The PWA and WPA had 5 billion dollars to spend.

Source H Which organisation has got these men back to work? What are they doing?

The Social Security Act, 1935

We take sickness and unemployment pay, pensions and the dole for granted. In America before 1935 there was no government scheme to provide these. The 1935 Act meant that workers and bosses could pay national insurance to provide sickness and unemployment pay and pensions for those people over 65.

Questions

1 Hold a competition to design logos like those in Source **G** to show the kind of work done by the FERA, the CWA, CCC, the PWA and the Social Security Act.

2 'The Banking Crisis': What did it mean? How did Roosevelt solve the problem?
If you had been able to interview one of the people in Source **B** at the time, and two years later in 1935, what might they have said about:
   - why they were in the crowd
   - the impact of Roosevelt shutting the banks (Source **C**)
   - what Roosevelt meant by his words in Source **A**
   - what they felt about the measures listed in the panel 'The New Deal – 100 days of action' on page 43, why they were passed, and their impact.

3 Prepare a 150-word report for a Russian (Communist) newspaper in 1934, saying how Roosevelt had solved the banking crisis. Mention:
   a) shutting the bank
   b) Roosevelt's speeches
   c) the CCC's impact on young people (Source **D**)
   d) the CWA's first thirty days, the work it continued to do, and how effective it was (Source **E**)
   e) the NIRA and the unions (Source **G**)
   f) the PWA's big projects
   g) the Social Security Act 1935.

Farming, 1933–36

▶ **How did the New Deal tackle the farming problem?**

What does Source **A** suggest happened to farming in the 1930s? The collapse of farm prices hit farmers hard. Many stopped working the land. Poor farmers grew the same crops year after year. The soil became poorer and poorer. In the early 1930s a drought gripped the Midwest. John Steinbeck wrote about it in a famous novel, *The Grapes of Wrath* (Source **B**).

Source A A farm in the Midwest. What has happened to this farm?

The Sun flared down on the growing corn day after day. The surface of the earth crusted, a thin hard crust, and as the sky became pale so the earth became pale. The air was thin and the sky more pale. In the roads where the teams of horses moved, where the wheels milled the ground the dirt crust broke and the dust formed. Every moving thing lifted the dust into the air. A walking man lifted a thin layer as high as his waist, and a wagon lifted the dust as high as the fence tops and an automobile trailed a cloud behind it. The dust was long in settling back again. When June was half gone the big clouds moved out of Texas. Then men in the fields looked up and sniffed at them. The clouds dropped a little spattering and hurried on to some other country.

Source B From John Steinbeck, *The Grapes of Wrath*, 1939

The drought gripped the states shown on Source **C**. A nightmare followed: the topsoil blew away and a 'Dustbowl' formed – see page 48.

The collapse in farm prices, the drought and the Dustbowl meant that many farmers were ruined.

● They owed money to the banks.
● The farmers could not pay.
● The banks took over their farms.
● The farmers and their families left their farms and took to the roads. Many moved west towards California looking for money, or poured into the cities and their shanty towns.

Government action

What did the government do to help the farmers? The key was to give farmers more cash for their crops and animals.

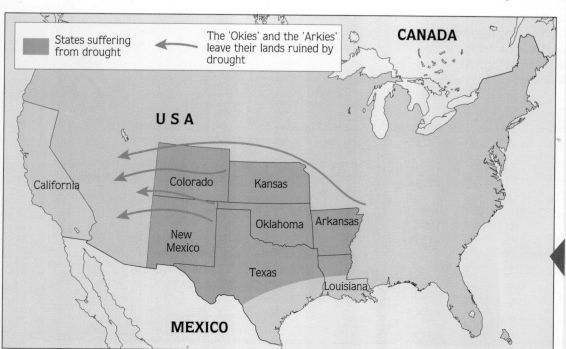

States suffering from drought

The 'Okies' and the 'Arkies' leave their lands ruined by drought

CANADA

USA

California
Colorado
Kansas
Oklahoma
Arkansas
New Mexico
Texas
Louisiana

MEXICO

Source C The 'Drought States' of the Midwest

The Farming Programme

- The **Farm Credit Administration (FCA)** gave $100 million in loans to farmers who owed money to the banks.
- The **Federal Security Administration (FSA)** gave grants at low rates of interest to enable many thousands of farmers to buy their farms.
- The **Agricultural Adjustment Administration (AAA)** granted subsidies to farmers to reduce production. In 1933 about 10 million acres of land were taken out of growing cotton, 8 million acres were taken out of growing wheat, and the tobacco harvest was cut by about one-third. In 1934 the AAA spent $120 million. This pushed up prices.
- The **Resettlement Administration (1935)** set up special camps for migrant farm workers to reduce the numbers ending up in Hoovervilles. It aimed to move farmers from areas with poor soil on to good land. The Resettlement Administration gave money to over 650,000 families. For many of the farmers who had lost their land it was too little, too late.
- The **Tennessee Valley Authority (TVA) 1933** was set up to deal with the problem of farming in the Tennessee Valley (Source **D**). Erosion here was widespread and huge numbers of farmers were leaving the land.
  - The TVA bought, built and ran dams for electric power and irrigation.
  - The dams controlled the flooding that swept away the rich topsoil.
  - The TVA sold cheap electricity from the dams to farms, homes and factories. Around 160 local electricity companies sold the electricity.
  - The electricity was used to make cheap fertiliser. The fertiliser helped make the land grow more crops. These crops in turn helped stop erosion.
  - The Authority opened up 1,000 kilometres of the Tennessee river to shipping. Massive locks were built to help long-distance barges carry the produce from the area to market.
  - The TVA gave help for planting forests on eroded land.
- To stop further soil erosion, the government planted huge areas of forest up to 150 kilometres wide, stretching from Texas to the borders of Canada.

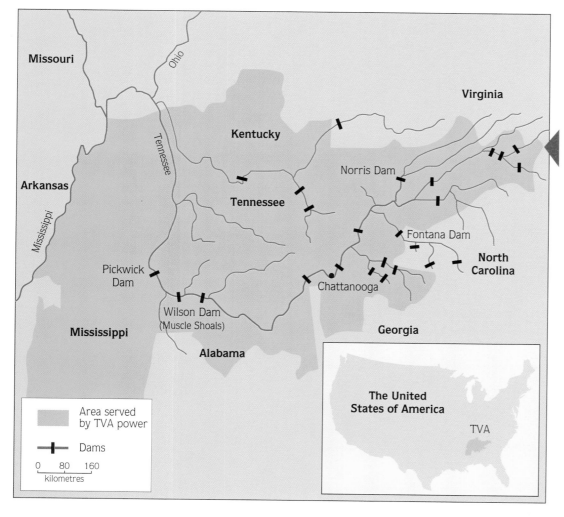

Source D The area covered by the Tennessee Valley Authority

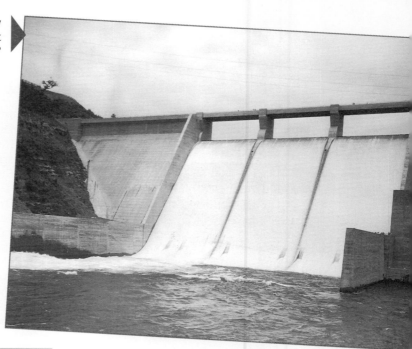

Source E Part of the Tennessee Valley Authority project. What does the photograph suggest about the scale of the TVA's work?

The Dustbowl and migration

The farmers worst hit by the disaster lived in the states of Texas, Colorado, Oklahoma, New Mexico and Kansas (see Source **C**). For years farmers in these states had been over-farming the land. By growing the same crops year after year they had slowly exhausted the soil. By grazing too many cattle they had gradually destroyed the pasture land, leaving the soil loose and broken. The drought described in Source **B** turned this broken soil to dust. Then between 1933 and 1935 strong winds swept across the huge area that had now become known as the 'Dustbowl' (Source **F**).

A gentle wind followed the rain clouds . . . It grew strong and hard. Little by little the sky was darkened by the rising dust which it loosened and carried away. The finest dust disappeared into the darkening sky. The dawn came but no day. In the grey sky a red sun appeared, a dim red circle that gave a little light, like dust . . . And the wind cried and whimpered over the fallen corn. Men and women huddled in their houses and they tied handkerchiefs over their noses and wore goggles to protect their eyes . . .

In the morning the dust hung like fog . . . An even blanket covered the earth. It settled on the corn, piled up on the tops of the fence posts, piled up on the wires. Men stood by their fences and looked at the ruined corn, dying fast now . . .

Source F From John Steinbeck, *The Grapes of Wrath*, 1939

Source G From John Steinbeck, *The Grapes of Wrath*, 1939

The owners of the land came out onto the land, or more often a spokesman for the owners came . . . And at last the owner men drove into the yards and sat in their cars to talk out of the windows . . . 'The tenant system won't work any more. One man on a tractor can take the place of 12 families. Pay him a wage and take all the crop. We have to do it.'

The tenant men looked up alarmed:

'But what'll happen to us? How'll we eat?' 'You'll have to get off the land. The ploughs will go through your farms.'

And now the tenant men stood up angrily:

'Grampa took up this land and he had to kill the Indians to drive them away . . . And Pa was born here . . . and we were born here. And Pa had to borrow money. The bank owned the land from then on – but we stayed and we got a little bit of what we raised.'

'We know all that. It's not us, it's the bank.'

'Sure,' cried the tenant men 'but it's our land! Even if it's no good it's still ours! We were born on it – that's what makes it ours being born on it, working on it, dying on it.'

'We're sorry,' said the owner men. 'Why don't you go on west to California? There's work out there and it never gets cold. Why, you can reach out anywhere and pick up an orange.'

Scientists believe that about 850 million tonnes of topsoil simply blew away. Some farmers in the Dustbowl lost all their topsoil. Others found their land covered in dust dunes. Nearly 4 million hectares of farmland were destroyed. Another 30 million hectares were damaged. Most small farmers and tenant farmers, already in debt, went bust. Only the big farmers could survive (Source **G**).

As they were forced off the land, hundreds of thousands of people packed everything they owned into old cars and trucks and set off West. Many had read handbills and seen movies about California. As soon as they left, their small farms disappeared. However, Steinbeck tells us there was no welcome for the newcomers in California (Source **H**).

Source H From John Steinbeck, *The Grapes of Wrath*, 1939

'She's a nice country. But she was stole a long time ago. You never will have seen such pretty country. And you'll pass land which is fine and flat with good water supplies and that land's not being used. But you can't have none of that land. That's Cattle Company land . . . You go in there and you plant a little corn and you'll go to jail. You never been called "Okie"?'

'Okie? What's that?'

'Well, "Okie" used to mean you were from Oklahoma. Now it means you're a dirty son-of-a-bitch. "Okie" means you're scum. I hear there's 300,000 of our people there and living like hog because everything in California is owned. There ain't nothing left.'

Source I From John Steinbeck, *The Grapes of Wrath*, 1939

When there was work for a man, ten men fought for it – fought with a low wage. 'If that fellow will work for 30 cents, I'll work for 25.'

'If he'll take 25, I'll do it for 20.'

'No, me. I'm hungry. I'll work for 15.'

'I'll work for food. The kids – you ought to see them. They're coming out in little boils. And they can't run around.'

And this was good, for wages went down and prices stayed up. The great land owners were glad and they sent out more hand bills to bring more people in. And pretty soon now we'll have serfs [slaves] again.

Most of the migrant farmers found little work in California and they ended up in Hoovervilles.

Source J
Migrants from the Dustbowl move west

Questions

1 a) Describe the scene in Source **A** as if you were walking round the farm.

b) Read Source **B** quickly. What words and phrases does Steinbeck use to convey what the drought was like, and what it meant to farmers? What might the 'walking man' have seen, smelled, felt and thought about his farm?

c) What happened to the farmers on farms like the one in Source **A**, who were ruined in the drought (Sources **B**, **F**, **G**)?

d) What do Sources **B–G** suggest about the extent and nature of the farming crisis?

e) How did the TVA deal with the farming problem (see the panel on 'The Farming Programme' and Sources **D** and **E**)?

f) What problems faced migrants when they reached California?

g) The extracts from Steinbeck are from a novel, *The Grapes of Wrath*.

- What problem is there in using a novel as a historical source?
- What evidence is there that the descriptions in the novel reflect reality?

2 In groups, create a drama. You represent a farming family in the TVA area in the 1930s. Work out what the characters were like, the situations they lived in, the problems they faced and how they coped with them. The drama should cover:

- life before the drought
- the impact of the Dustbowl
- how the family and other families reacted
- the TVA measures and how they changed life on the farm
- what happened to neighbours who left to go to California.

Opposition to the New Deal, 1935–36

Why was the New Deal opposed?
What form did the opposition take?

Roosevelt made many enemies, both Democrats and Republicans. Huey Long was a threat in the Democratic party. Why?

Huey Long

One of FDR's main opponents in the Democratic Party was Senator Huey Long of Louisiana. He wanted to go much further than Roosevelt in using the state's power to end the Depression.

Long's programme of state help for the poor in Louisiana put many back to work. In 1935 FDR got Congress to agree to a wealth tax, which Huey Long had been demanding for years.

However, Long did not live long enough to become a serious danger to either Roosevelt or American democracy. On 8 September 1935, a young doctor shot him in the stomach in the Louisiana state capitol building in Baton Rouge. Long died the following day.

The Republican attack on the New Deal

What were the attacks on the New Deal about? Many Republicans thought the New Deal was dangerous.

Source A From Alden P. Hatch, *Franklin D. Roosevelt*

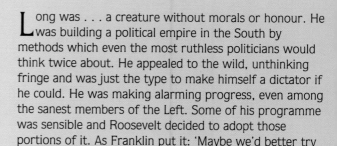

Long was . . . a creature without morals or honour. He was building a political empire in the South by methods which even the most ruthless politicians would think twice about. He appealed to the wild, unthinking fringe and was just the type to make himself a dictator if he could. He was making alarming progress, even among the sanest members of the Left. Some of his programme was sensible and Roosevelt decided to adopt those portions of it. As Franklin put it: 'Maybe we'd better try to steal some of Huey's thunder.'

The US Government was now taking part in the everyday life of Americans in a way that it had never done before. Some feared that this could bring about a dictatorship (one-man or one-party rule) in America. Many businessmen believed that the government should keep out of business affairs. They saw government-run projects such as the Tennessee Valley Authority as the 'thin end of the wedge', leading to more and more taxation and corruption.

Huey Long

- **1893** Huey Long was born the son of a poor farmer.

- **1917** He was elected to the post of Louisiana Railroad Commissioner. Long saw himself as leader of the poor whites of the Deep South and spoke out against the power of big business.

- **1928** He was elected Governor of Louisiana and began a programme of state spending on schools, roads and other projects.

- **1930** Long was elected to the US Senate. He promised that if he became President he would bring in food

subsidies and confiscate [take away] all private fortunes over $3 million, giving $5,000 of the money to every family in America. But he did not explain how this was to be achieved.

- **1935** Long was assassinated. Many Americans felt they were well rid of a dangerous man. Others pointed out that Long had reduced unemployment in Louisiana, and he had many supporters among the poor whites.

Source B Roosevelt, the enemy of the rich. What is the cartoon saying about how Roosevelt is running America?

Source C President Roosevelt held regular press conferences (meetings with reporters) to get his ideas across to the American people

Roosevelt and socialism

Some people thought that if Roosevelt was not stopped, America would end up with a socialist or communist system where the government owns and runs all businesses. As Republican Frank Knox said, 'The New Deal candidate has been leading us toward Moscow.'

Source D Comment by Congressman Martin Dies

Stalin [the communist leader of the USSR] has baited his hook with a 'progressive' worm and the New Deal suckers swallowed it bait, hook, line and sinker.'

Worker power

Business also feared that Roosevelt's new industrial laws (see pages 43–45) gave too much power to American workers.

Growth in the civil service

Other Republicans pointed to the fact that under Roosevelt the size of the Government was growing quickly. In 1932 there were 500,000 US civil servants. By 1939 there would be 920,000.

Morally wrong

FDR's enemies also argued that parts of the New Deal were morally wrong.

- For instance, the Agricultural Adjustment Administration's policies (see page 47) meant that thousands of farmers were paid to destroy their crops and plough them back into the ground as a means of keeping up prices.
- Republicans said this was a terrible thing to do at a time when many Americans were going hungry.
- Some of Roosevelt's opponents were also against social security for the unemployed, and against old age pensions. They felt that these measures could lead to Americans 'going soft' or being less keen to work hard.

Eleanor Roosevelt

Others did not like the way the President's wife Eleanor spoke out for the poor and the unemployed. They said that she should not take part in political affairs but simply remain at her husband's side. Roosevelt was attacked by conservative Republicans and Democrats for going too far, and by liberal Democrats for not going far enough. The Old South seemed to be getting little from the New Deal, southern blacks least of all.

Roosevelt and the Supreme Court

In America the Supreme Court can decide whether an Act of Congress is legal or not. The nine judges of the Court were mainly old and conservative. In 1935 the Court declared that the Agricultural Adjustment Act and the National Industrial Recovery Act were 'unconstitutional'.

FDR believed the Supreme Court judges had made these decisions simply because they did not like the laws rather than because the laws went against the Constitution.

The President tried to get Congress to agree to allow him to appoint up to six new judges of his choice. There was an uproar – his enemies said Roosevelt was acting like Hitler or Stalin! Many Americans felt that Roosevelt was now trying to tamper with the Constitution to give himself more power, and he lost a lot of popular support (Source **F**).

Congress refused to agree to the President's demands. However, the Supreme Court judges seemed to have learned their lesson. From then on they were much more cautious about declaring FDR's New Deal laws 'unconstitutional'.

The 1936 presidential election

Despite its success, the New Deal made FDR many enemies. Leading Republicans were determined that he should not win the 1936 election. During the campaign FDR hit back at his critics.

Source G Alden P. Hatch, *Franklin D. Roosevelt*

Source E What the Supreme Court said about the NIRA

We are of the opinion that such an attempt to fix the hours and wages of workers was not a lawful use of government power.

Source F Cartoon by J. H. 'Ding' Darling. The compass is the Supreme Court, Congress is the figure at the bottom of the picture. What does the cartoon tell us about how the newspaper in which it appeared saw Roosevelt?

THAT COMPASS DOESN'T POINT THE WAY I WANT TO GO. CHANGE IT. NOW!

They [the big businessmen] had begun to consider the government of the United States as a mere limb of their own affairs. We now know that government by organised money is just as dangerous as government by an organised mob. Never before in all our history have these forces been so united against one candidate as they stand today. They are united in their hate for me and I welcome their hatred.

Landslide! The voters swept Roosevelt back into power as President in 1936.

Source H

20 January 1937

Franklin D. Roosevelt began his second term as President today . . . 'In this nation,' he cried over the drumming of rain on umbrellas, 'I see millions denied education, recreation, and the opportunity to better their lot and the lot of their children. I see one-third of a nation ill-housed, ill-clad, ill-nourished.'

Source I From Ronald Reagan, *An American Life*, 1990

Source J Ronald Reagan as a young man

However, opposition to the New Deal did not end when Roosevelt was re-elected. In the 1930s the film star Ronald Reagan was a Democrat and a strong supporter of Roosevelt. As the years went by Reagan changed his mind and came to believe that the New Deal was damaging America. When Reagan himself was elected President in 1980, he saw it as his job to cut government welfare spending and to try to 'undo' the New Deal. Source **I** is from his autobiography.

Like my brother Jack – and millions of other Americans – I worshipped FDR. He'd entered the White House facing a national emergency as grim as any the country has ever faced and, acting quickly, he had put in place a plan of action to deal with the crisis.

During his fireside chats, his strong, gentle, confident voice brought comfort and strength to a nation caught up in a storm. He reassured us that we could lick any problem. I will never forget that.

But many people forget Roosevelt ran for President promising to cut waste in government. One of his sons, Franklin Roosevelt Jnr, often told me that his father had said many times his welfare and relief programmes during the Depression were meant only as emergency, stopgap measures to cope with a crisis. He did not mean to plant the seeds of a permanent welfare state. Government giveaway programmes, FDR said, 'destroy the human spirit,' and he was right. As smart as he was, though, I suspect even FDR didn't realise that once you created a bureaucracy [lots of government officials], it took on a life of its own. It was almost impossible to close down a bureaucracy once it had been created.

Meanwhile, as Roosevelt started his second term as President, America was facing a new economic slump.

Questions

1 a) Why was Huey Long a threat to Roosevelt?
b) Why did Republicans hate the New Deal?
c) What was the quarrel with the Supreme Court about?
d) Why did Roosevelt win the 1936 presidential election so easily?

2 Look back to the 'Beating the Depression' box on page 41. How would 'your' family vote in the election, and why? Consider its views about:
  • Huey Long's ideas
  • the New Deal programme and how successful it has been
  • Roosevelt's attack on the Supreme Court

  • FDR's election campaign.
Hold an election meeting in which each family puts forward its views.

3 a) Write a poem or short play or produce a set of cartoons with titles, captions and notes on what they show, describing the New Deal and the Depression from the viewpoint of 'your' American family in 1936.
b) Create a class display of poems, plays and cartoons.

4 Look at Source **I**.
a) In what ways did Reagan admire Roosevelt?
b) What criticisms does Reagan make of Roosevelt's policies?
c) Which criticisms do you agree with?

The New Deal – success or failure?

▶ **How serious was the New Slump?**
How successful was the New Deal?

The New Slump, 1937–38

The New Deal failed to end the Depression (Source **A**). From 1936 Roosevelt had run out of ideas on how to find work for the millions without jobs. It took another World War to boost government spending to a level that would bring back full employment to America.

In August 1937, support for Roosevelt dropped sharply when the US economy slumped into a new depression. Within a year unemployment had risen by 2.5 million. In April 1938 FDR started a new spending programme. But a year later there were still more than ten million people unemployed (Source **B**).

Source A A billboard or hoarding that could be seen in America in the late 1930s. What does this photograph suggest about the success of the New Deal?

Source B
Unemployment during the New Deal ▶

Year	Unemployed in millions	% of workforce out of work
1933	13	25
1934	11	22
1935	11	20
1936	9	17
1937	8	14
1938	10	19
1939	9	17

From *History of the 20th Century*, Phoebus Publishing 1976

The recession of 1937–38

Roosevelt got some of his New Deal ideas from the British economist John Maynard Keynes. Keynes believed that government action was the key to ending the Depression. Keynes argued that:

- Western governments should increase their spending on public works such as roads, railways and building programmes
- this extra spending would create millions of new jobs
- the new workers would have more money to spend on goods such as clothing, radios, refrigerators, etc.
- the industries producing these goods would need to take on more workers who, in turn, would have more spending power
- this would lead to yet more industries expanding and taking on more workers
- all the new workers would be paying more taxes, so in the end the government would get most of its money back.

We can show these ideas as a diagram (Source **C**). Keynes believed that only government spending could reverse the 'downward spiral' (see page 37).

Source C How to end the Depression, according to Keynes

The balanced budget

FDR did not believe that a government could go on spending more than it got back in taxes for ever. He said that one day the government would have to 'balance the budget'.

- In 1937 the US government deficit (debt) reached $4 billion.
- Keynes urged the President to increase government spending still further.
- But FDR thought this was 'against common sense'.
- Instead, he slashed public spending, putting the US economy back on the downward spiral until April 1938.

1937 and 1938 were also years of industrial conflict.

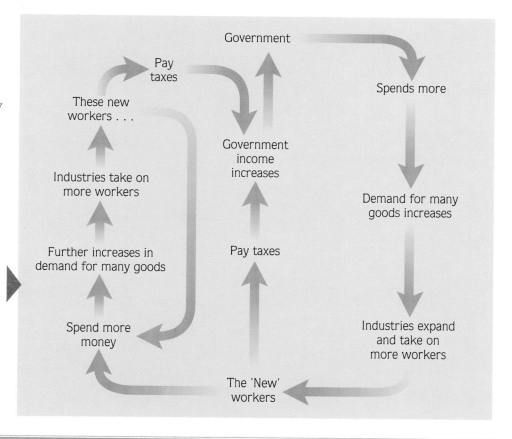

Industrial conflict

- After the passing of the National Industrial Relations Act and the setting up of the National Recovery Board, millions of workers joined trade unions for the first time.
- The newly-formed Congress of Industrial Organisations (CIO) led by John Lewis had strongly supported FDR's election campaign in 1936.
- In 1937 the CIO started a series of sit-down strikes in many of America's largest companies, including US

Steel, Ford, General Motors and General Electric. The workers struck for better pay.

- The companies hit back by trying to employ strike-breakers to do the work instead. This led to rioting in many factories. The worst violence took place at the Republic Steel Company in Chicago between May and July 1937. The fighting there was more like a war than an industrial dispute (Sources **D** and **E**).

Source D Press reports describing events in the Republic Steel Company dispute

30 May 1937
Sheet and Tube factory

Guards fired on strikers from trucks, killing two and wounding dozens. On the same day, 400 miles away in South Chicago, 160 police confronted 1,500 pickets at a Republic plant. The strikers wielded car cranks, bolts and bricks; the police had guns. After the shooting, 10 strikers lay dead; of the 78 injured, 5 were police.

4 July 1937

Eighteen strikers are dead, 10 of them shot down here on Memorial Day. Thousands are streaming back to work, and still the steel union leaders refuse to admit defeat. But resolve on the picket lines has worn thin. A compromise offered July 1 at Inland Steel brought hungry strikers back to work without even a contract guarantee.

Source E A victim of the labour dispute. What is happening to the chief of Ford security in this picture?

Source F Frankenstein, a trade union leader who was beaten up by security guards at the Ford factory. Why do you think he has been beaten up?

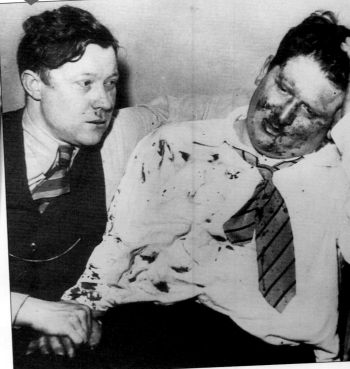

Unionists 'sat in' factories while they were on strike. Company managers found that they could not break the sit-down strikes without seeing their factories wrecked in the process.

FDR refused to get involved, and in most cases the unions won better pay for their workers. Most unions have given their support to the Democratic Party ever since.

Fair Labour Standards Act, 1938
FDR got Congress to pass the Fair Labour Standards Act to tighten up the law against child labour and to establish a national minimum wage for all those working in interstate business. This was the last important measure of the New Deal. The President's time was increasingly being taken up with foreign affairs, as another World War seemed more and more likely.

The 1940 election

In 1940 Roosevelt was the first President to stand for a third term in office. He was re-elected, but only just. Why was he re-elected (Source **G**)?

Meanwhile Europe was at war. The rest of Roosevelt's life would be taken up with the Second World War.

Judgement on the New Deal

Source H From Alistair Cooke, *America*, 1973

1935

Congress disbursed relief funds in floods. Roosevelt had in the meantime shoved through Congress huge federal loans for public works, and at the same time he gave the industrial workers who had been hounded by company spies the right to organise and bargain. He handed out hard dollars to the unemployed and took three million youngsters off the streets to build highways and plant ten million trees. He mobilized actors in a federal theatre and, in the happiest inspiration of the Works Progress Administration, hired unemployed scholars, writers, and local historians to produce several hundred volumes of guidebooks to the states. He stopped the automatic production of groaning farm surpluses, paid the Southern farmers to diversify their crops and built enormous dams to hold the flooding of the great river valleys – and then made the valleys flower through electricity and controlled irrigation. In all he brought national relief to national unemployment; he conserved the soil of the worn-out South; he established once for all the federal government's right to plan economic and social welfare on a national scale.

Source G From a Boston newspaper, November 1940

Out of the population of 30,000, hundreds got pay rises under the wage-hour law. Hundreds of seasonal workers are helped out in the slack months by unemployment benefits. The NYA is helping 300–500 youths; at the worst of the Depression thousands held WPA jobs. Six hundred old people receive old age pensions and another 600 get aid for dependent children. Charlestown is a depressed area. The WPA improved its bathing beach. A new low-cost housing project will relieve some of the area's overcrowding.

The box suggests why the New Deal was important.

The importance of the New Deal

1 Hundreds of thousands of square miles of ruined farmland were reclaimed and thousands of square miles added to the national parks.

2 Jobs were created for millions of desperate people and help given to the poor.

3 The power of the President greatly increased.

4 The United States Government accepted that it must be partly responsible for the welfare, health and security of all American citizens.

5 The government became more involved in business affairs and in the daily lives of ordinary Americans.

6 The power of the Federal Government over the state governments increased.

7 The New Deal enabled the American system of government to survive.

Questions

1 **a)** What ideas about the New Deal might the photographer of Source **A** want you to have?
b) Does Source **B** support the idea that the New Deal was a success?
c) What happened to the strikers in Source **E**?
d) What does the text and Sources **E**, **F** and **G** tell you about industrial relations in America in the 1930s?
e) List all the points which the extracts in Sources **G** and **H** favour. Which do you think are the most important?
f) In your own words, explain the views of John Maynard Keynes (page 55). In what ways did they differ from those of FDR?

2 In groups of four, take the following roles:
• a rich Republican banker from New York who owns a steel company
• a poor farmer from the area of the TVA
• a trade union leader in the iron and steel industry
• a loyal member of FDR's government.
Discuss what each of you would have to say about the following:
a) accusations that FDR was a Communist
b) the growth of government power since 1933
c) social welfare and unemployment support
d) the work of the NRA
e) the Supreme Court Crisis of 1936
f) the problem of strikes
g) the Fair Labour Standards Act
h) the 1937 recession
i) the importance of the New Deal.

5 America and the Second World War

The arsenal of democracy

 How was America the 'arsenal of democracy'?

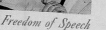

OURS...to fight for

Freedom of Speech *Freedom of...*

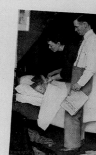

Freedom from Want *Freedom from...*

Source B
'The four freedoms'

Isolation

When the Second World War broke out in Europe in September 1939, most Americans strongly believed that the United States should keep out of the war. Ever since 1919 American Presidents had stuck to the policy of isolation. President Roosevelt had watched the rise of Nazi Germany and a warlike Japan with growing concern. But, like the British and French governments, he had done little about it. With the outbreak of the Second World War in September 1939, Roosevelt at last got Congress to agree to big increases in defence spending. America was in danger!

Britain and America

The British began buying American war materials on a large scale, as they had done in the First World War.

By the summer of 1940 Britain stood alone against the huge new Nazi empire, facing a likely German invasion at any time. Many people now feared what would happen if Britain was defeated.

Source A From the *New York Times*, 1940

> Were the control of the seas by Britain lost, the Atlantic would no longer be an obstacle – rather it would become a broad highway for the conqueror moving westwards. There is no escape in isolation. We have only two choices: we surrender or we can do our part in holding the line.

Millions of Americans admired the way the British refused to give in and they were stirred by the fighting speeches of Winston Churchill.

American industries expanded rapidly to supply the British war effort. By the end of 1940 unemployment in the United States had fallen to eight million. Meanwhile Roosevelt had handed over 50 old destroyers to the British Royal Navy in return for bases in Newfoundland and the Caribbean.

Lend–Lease

As he started his third term as President, FDR asked Congress to support all countries that were fighting in defence of 'The Four Freedoms' (Source **B**). In March 1941 Roosevelt got Congress to pass the Lend–Lease Act. This said that America would 'lend' Britain the supplies to fight the war. In another radio broadcast FDR explained how this worked (Source **C**).

> Suppose my neighbour's home catches fire, and I have a length of garden hose. I don't say to him 'Neighbour my garden hose cost me $15 so you have to give me $15 for it.' I don't want $15 – I want my garden hose back after the fire is over . . . But suppose it gets smashed up during the fire? . . . My neighbour says: 'Alright, I will replace it.'

Source C FDR explains the Lend–Lease Act, in a radio broadcast, 1941

In March 1941 America had lent Britain $7,000 million to buy US weapons. By December 1941 unemployment had fallen by another 2.5 million. Roosevelt announced that the United States would be 'The arsenal of democracy'.

When Hitler invaded the USSR in June 1941, Lend–Lease was extended to the Russians. By the end of the war $50,000 million had been supplied to America's allies.

Pearl Harbor, 7 December 1941

On 7 December Japanese planes bombed American warships peacefully at anchor in the American base at Pearl Harbor. So ended American neutrality. Following the Japanese attack, on 11 December Germany and Italy – Japan's allies – declared war on America.

The American war effort

Roosevelt and Churchill met often during the war to plan a joint campaign. Even though for several months Americans on the west coast feared a Japanese invasion, the two leaders agreed to put the defeat of Germany first.

In 1941 Roosevelt set up the War Production Board. American industry was put on a war footing and production soared. In 1941 the United States had built less than 20,000 war planes (Source **D**).

In 1943 over 90,000 planes were built. By the end of the war American machine tool production was over seven times greater than it had been in 1939. In 1945 the United States produced more iron and steel than the whole world had made in 1939. Between 1939 and 1945 US industrial production doubled.

The impact of war

The Second World War put an end to unemployment in the United States. All men between 18 and 45 were conscripted into the armed forces (if they passed the medical). Women had to do the jobs men had done before 1939 (Source **E**). By 1945 over 15 million Americans were in uniform. During the war 290,000 Americans were killed and 670,000 were wounded.

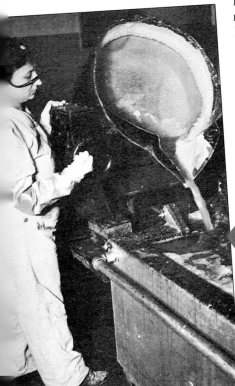

Source E Women took over men's jobs during the war. This woman is working in a munitions factory.

In the countryside outside Detroit there was a creek running through flat sandy farming land. Within six months of Pearl Harbor this scene had been changed into what somebody called: 'the most enormous room in the history of man'. It was half a mile long and quarter of a mile wide. Raw materials were fed in at one end and came out an hour later at the other end in the shape of a finished bomber. This was plucked by another assembly line and moved out for immediate testing on an airfield.

Source D Alistair Cooke, *America*, 1973

Very few of these were civilians. American civilians suffered less in the war than in any other country. American cities were not bombed and the standard of living for many Americans rose during the war.

The war brought other changes: over 27 million Americans moved home between 1941 and 1945, more than at any other time in American history. Not all moved out of choice – 112,000 Japanese-Americans, living mainly in the west, were interned (put into prison camps).

Roosevelt's death

In 1944 Roosevelt was re-elected for a fourth term as President but he was clearly a very sick man. The strain of leading his country through the greatest depression and the greatest war in history had been too much. In April 1945, as the war in Europe was coming to an end, Franklin Roosevelt died.

Truman and the end of the war

The war in the Pacific was fiercely fought. American forces slowly moved from island to island, driving the Japanese back with appalling losses on both sides. To end the war the new President, Harry S. Truman, ordered the dropping of atomic bombs on the Japanese cities of Hiroshima and Nagasaki in August 1945.

Questions

1 a) Why did public support for Britain grow?
 b) Put the argument in the *New York Times* (Source **A**) into your own words.
 c) What was Lend–Lease?
 d) What was the importance of Pearl Harbor?
 e) List five ways in which the United States became the 'arsenal of democracy'.
 f) What impact did the war have on America?

2 Use the evidence in this section and any other sources you can find (books, magazines, etc.) to write a 200-word obituary on Franklin D. Roosevelt.

6 Post-war America

The end of isolationism

Why did America not return to isolationism?
Why did relations with Russia collapse and the Cold War begin?

Franklin D. Roosevelt

We seek peace – enduring peace. More than an end to war we want an end to the beginnings of all wars. We must develop the ability for all peoples, of all kinds, to live together and work together in the same world, at peace – I ask you to keep up your faith.

Roosevelt was dying The last words he wrote (Source **A**) meant that the USA and the USSR should get along together and prevent war. At the Yalta Conference in February 1945, the United States, the USSR and Great Britain had agreed:
- to set up a United Nations Organisation
- to divide Germany, Austria and the city of Berlin into four zones (American, Soviet, French and British)
- that free elections should be held in all the countries liberated by the Allies, including the countries of Eastern Europe freed from the Nazis by the Red Army.

The United Nations

At first things seemed to go well. In April 1945 America, Britain and Russia set up the United Nations. The UN Charter said that the aim of the UN was 'to save the future generations from the scourge of war'. In July 1945 the Senate agreed to US membership of the United Nations.

America and Russia quarrel over Europe

However, over the future of Germany and Eastern Europe, divisions between the USA and the USSR were already showing. While the Western powers set about rebuilding their zones of Germany, the Russians stripped their zone of anything they could use to re-build the USSR (Sources **B** and **C**).

"IF WE DON'T LET HIM WORK, WHO'S GOING TO KEEP HIM?"

Source B What point is this cartoon making?

Source C Entry in the diary of James Forrestal, Truman's Secretary for Defence, on 20 April 1945

I saw the US Ambassador to Russia last night. He stated his fears about our future relations with them unless we showed much greater firmness. He said that using the fear of Germany as an excuse, they would continue to set up Communist governments in the countries around their borders. He said the outward thrust of Communism was not dead and that it might become as dangerous as Nazism.

It soon became clear to the American government that Stalin's aim was to set up Communist governments in all the countries of Eastern Europe under Red Army control (Sources **D**, **E** and **F**).

Source D Europe in 1946

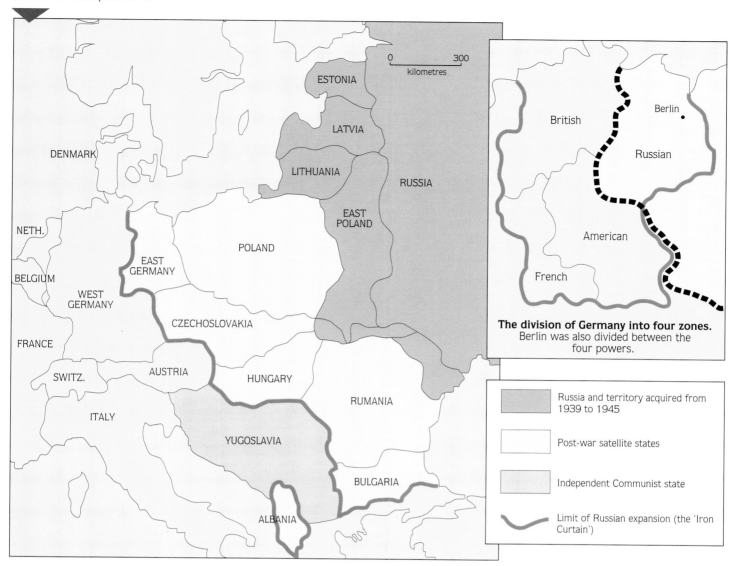

The division of Germany into four zones.
Berlin was also divided between the four powers.

Russia and territory acquired from 1939 to 1945

Post-war satellite states

Independent Communist state

Limit of Russian expansion (the 'Iron Curtain')

Source E Stalin's reply to Truman's call early in 1946 for free elections in Hungary, Romania and Bulgaria

> Any freely elected government in these countries will be anti-Soviet government and we cannot allow that.

Source F Truman, writing to his Secretary of State

> Unless Russia is faced with an iron fist and strong language another war is in the making. Only one language do they understand: 'How many divisions have you?' I'm tired of babying the Soviets.

The Iron Curtain

However, short of war there was little the United States could do to stop Russia from making Eastern Europe Communist, even though at that time the United States was the only country with the atomic bomb.

Source G Winston Churchill addresses the American people at Fulton, Missouri in March 1946

> A shadow has fallen upon the Allied victory. From Stettin in the Baltic to Trieste in the Adriatic, an iron curtain has fallen across the continent. Behind that line all the states of Central and Eastern Europe are being controlled from Moscow. This is not the liberated Europe we fought to build, nor is it one which contains what is needed for lasting peace.

In 1947, faced with the danger of Communist guerrillas taking over Greece and Turkey, the President announced what was to become known as the 'Truman Doctrine'. It was the opposite of isolationism (Source **H**).

Not everyone agreed with this policy (Source **I**).

Source H   The Truman Doctrine

We are willing to help free peoples to keep their freedom and their independence against aggressive movements that seek to force totalitarian governments [where a government seeks total control over people's lives] on them. I believe it must be the policy of the United States to support free peoples who are resisting attacks by armed minorities or outside pressures.

Source I   Former Vice-President Harry Wallace addresses a packed meeting in Madison Square Gardens, New York

We are here tonight to state that the Truman Doctrine endangers peace. Our soldiers did not win one war to fight another. Our workers and farmers toiled for freedom not for fear. The world is hungry. The world cries out, not for American tanks and guns to destroy more lives and leave more hunger, but for American food to fulfil the promise of peace . . . Our banks will give dollars and our arsenals will give weapons. When that is not enough our people will be asked to give their sons.

The Marshall Plan

Truman's Secretary of State, George Marshall, realised that stopping the spread of Communism would take more than the Truman Doctrine. Something more positive was needed. By 1947 the economies of many West European countries were close to collapse (Source **J**).

Source K   George Marshall. What do his clothes and his general appearance suggest about his character?

Source J   George Marshall, speaking at Harvard University in June 1947

Raw materials and machinery are in short supply all over Europe. Machinery is lacking or worn out. Meanwhile people in the cities are short of food and fuel. Governments are forced to spend what little money they have in buying these things from abroad. The truth of the matter is that Europe's requirements for the next three or four years of foreign food and other essential products are far greater than her ability to pay. Our policy is directed against hunger, poverty, despair and chaos. Its purpose should be the revival of a working economy in the world so as to permit the growth of conditions in which free governments can exist.

George Marshall said that the United States should give billions of dollars in aid to help the countries of Europe and elsewhere recover from the war. However, many Congressmen were against the Marshall Plan. They did not think the United States could afford to do this. They feared it could lead to a new depression in the United States as well.

1948 The Cold War worsens

Most of these critics changed their minds in 1948 after a Communist take-over in Czechoslovakia, and signs that the Communists were going to do well in future elections in Italy. Congress passed the Foreign Assistance Act, giving an immediate grant of $5.3 billion to the countries of Western Europe. In all, nearly $15 billion was given by the United States to other countries in Marshall Aid. It was the biggest foreign aid programme in history and brought about the recovery of Western Europe.

Stalin claimed that Marshall Aid was simply aimed at making Western Europe depend completely on the United States.

Source L The Berlin airlift. What might these people be thinking as they watch the aeroplanes flying into and out of Berlin?

The Berlin blockade

In 1948 Stalin responded by trying to force the United States, Britain and France to give up their zones in Berlin. All Berlin's road and rail links with the West were blocked off by Soviet troops. The Western allies responded by airlifting supplies into the city (Source L). For a while many feared that another World War would break out.

Even before Stalin called off the blockade in 1949, most of the countries of Western Europe and North America had set up the North Atlantic Treaty Organisation (NATO) to defend themselves against Russian attack.

In the same year the USSR tested its own atom bomb and an arms race with the USSR began. The reversal of isolationism was complete.

---

1 a) What did the Allies decide at the Yalta Conference?
b) What was the main aim of the United Nations?
c) What was the main point that Forrestal made (Source **C**)?
d) What threat does the text and Source **D** suggest Russia posed to Europe?
e) What did the dropping of the Iron Curtain mean (Source **G**)?
f) How was the Russians' treatment of their German zone different from that of the Americans, British and French?
g) What was the Truman Doctrine (Source **H**)? Why was it opposed (Source **I**)?
h) What was the point of the Marshall Plan (Source **J**)? Did it succeed?
i) How did Stalin react to Truman's call for free elections in East European countries?

j) What was the Berlin blockade (Source **L**)?
k) How did the North Atlantic Treaty Organisation reverse pre-1941 American foreign policy?
l) How important was the atom bomb to Russia?

2 Create a timeline of the main events in America's foreign policy from 1945 to 1949.

3 Write a short essay on *either* 'Why did America not return to isolationism?' *or* 'Why did relations with Russia collapse and the Cold War begin?'
Consider the argument you will use in your essay, and what point of view you will take. Mention:
- hopes in 1945, and the United Nations
- confrontation in Europe
- the Truman Doctrine
- the Marshall Plan
- the Berlin blockade.

The anti-Communist witch hunt, 1946–54

What caused the anti-Communist witch hunt in America after 1945?
What form did it take?
What role did Joseph McCarthy play?

Witches

From 1550 to 1700, many women were accused of witchcraft, jailed, tried, found guilty and burnt at the stake. Why do you think witch hunters picked on them? Some of the worst witch hunts took place in Massachusetts in the 1690s. History repeated itself 250 years later.

Joseph McCarthy – witch hunter

In 1946 Joseph McCarthy of Wisconsin was elected to the United States Senate (Source **A**). McCarthy played on people's fears and prejudices to start a 'witch hunt' of his own against Communists. After the Second World War, as one East European country after another fell under Soviet control, people like McCarthy said Communists were a threat to America's future.

Communists in the civil service

McCarthy and others claimed that there were people in the civil service who secretly supported the USSR. President Truman came under pressure to do something. Truman's enemies said he was 'soft on Communism'.

So Truman issued Executive Order 9835, which started a review of 'loyalty' in the civil service. The review resulted in 212 people being sacked from their jobs. None of them was ever charged with any crime.

The 'Red Scare' got even worse in 1949, when Communists came to power in China and the USSR detonated its own atom bomb.

On 20 February McCarthy repeated his claims in the US Senate.

- McCarthy did not give the names of any of the people on the list.
- Instead, his supporters got Congress to pass the McCarron-Nixon Internal Security Act. This said that all Communist organisations had to register with the government, and Communist supporters could have their passports taken away.
- Truman vetoed the Act, but Congress overruled him.

Source A Senator Joseph McCarthy. From this photograph, what sort of a man do you think he was?

Source B Senator McCarthy, speaking to the Women's Club of Wheeling, West Virginia on 9 February 1950

When a great democracy is destroyed it will not be because of the enemies from outside, but rather because of enemies within. At the end of the War we were the strongest nation on earth and morally the most powerful. Yet instead of being a beacon in the desert of destruction we have failed miserably . . . because of the traitors who have been treated so well by this nation. Those who have been selling this nation out have the finest jobs in Government. In my opinion the State Department . . . is thoroughly infested with Communists.

I have in my hand 57 cases of individuals who would appear to be either card-carrying members or certainly loyal to the Communist Party, but who nevertheless are still helping to shape our foreign policy. We are not just dealing with spies. We are dealing with a far more sinister type of activity because it permits the enemy to guide and shape our policy.

The Korean War

The McCarthy witch hunt gained strength in 1950 when Communist North Korea invaded South Korea. US troops were sent to Korea as part of what was officially a United Nations force. However, it soon became clear that the war would not be won with a few quick victories. Instead it became a stalemate, especially after Communist China joined in to support the North Koreans. The war dragged on until 1953 when Korea was permanently divided into two countries.

The attack on McCarthy

Meanwhile, in 1950 a Senate committee, chaired by Senator Millard Tydings, reported on McCarthy's claims (Source **C**).

Source C A Senate committee's opinion of McCarthy's claims

> A fraud and a hoax on the Senate of the United States and on the American people. They represent perhaps the most terrible campaign of half-truths and untruths in the history of the Republic.

McCarthy fights back

McCarthy simply accused the Tydings Committee of supporting Communists and continued with his campaign.

Source D Margaret Truman, in her biography of her father, describing the 1950 Senate elections

> Millard Tydings lost his seat in one of the most disgusting election campaigns in American history. The really evil genius in that election was Joe McCarthy and his supporters who gave out faked pictures supposedly showing Senator Tydings chatting with Earl Browder, the head of the Communist Party. It was a triumph of hatred and fear.

McCarthy's claims

As US forces suffered defeats in the Korean War and the fighting reached stalemate, McCarthy claimed that Communist spies were to blame for the setbacks. McCarthy even accused George Marshall of being a Communist plotter (Source **E**). Alsom McCarthy claimed that the Pentagon (the centre of US defence) was bugging his offices.

Source E Margaret Truman, on the situation in 1951

> Joe McCarthy spewed lies and slanders on dozens of reputations. He reached his peak on 14 June 1951 when he gave a 60,000 word speech in the Senate that attacked General George Marshall as a Communist plotter. For Dad this was the most hateful of the Senator's many slanders. That a man who had devoted his entire life to the service of his country could be smeared as a traitor in the Senate of the United States was almost unbelievable to Dad. In his press conference a few days later he treated the charge with contempt and said 'No comment!'

Many leading Americans were afraid to speak out against McCarthy in case he turned his attack on them. Others saw a chance to further their own career.

The 1952 presidential election

In the presidential election of 1952, Dwight Eisenhower and Richard Nixon supported McCarthy's campaign against Communist plotters. The witch hunt spread beyond government and the civil service. People sometimes found themselves sacked from their jobs if they were suspected of supporting Communism. Some writers and actors were 'black-listed' because of their political views. Source **F** shows McCarthy supporters on their way to a rally.

Source F Public support for McCarthy. What points are McCarthy's supporters making?

Eisenhower's new attack on civil servants

When he became President, Eisenhower ordered a new investigation into the civil service, saying that anyone who was thought to be a security risk would be dismissed. Between May 1953 and October 1954, 6,926 government workers lost their jobs (Source **G**). None of them was ever put on trial.

McCarthy had gone too far. In 1954 he accused 45 army officers of being Communist agents and managed to get the Communist Party banned in the United States (Source **H**).

The Republicans combed the government files attempting to dredge up charges against everyone in Dad's Administration. They found nothing. Even worse was the attempt to make out that Dad had something to do with Communism. The House of Representatives Un-American Activities Committee [set up in 1938] actually sent Dad a summons to testify in the case of one of his government aides who had been accused of being a Communist. He rejected the summons with the scorn it deserved. 'I have been accused, in effect,' he said on television, 'of knowingly betraying the security of the United States. This charge is of course false.' For once most of the newspapers were on Dad's side.

Source G Margaret Truman, on this period of her father's Presidency

Source H McCarthy accused US Army officers of being 'reds'

The televised Senate hearings

The Senate hearings that examined the charges against the officers were shown on television. Millions of people saw McCarthy abusing and bullying officers and civil servants. The public turned against him. The Senate passed a motion censuring McCarthy for 'improper conduct'.

Source I At a news conference, McCarthy accuses the US Army of trying to blackmail him into calling off his investigations into Communists in the Army.

The witch hunt ends

With the end of the Korean War and as relations with the USSR improved, Americans were less interested in Communist plots. McCarthy continued with his campaign until he died, in 1957, but people took less and less notice.

The witch hunt was over but some of the effects of McCarthyism can still be seen. If you ever want to visit the United States you will probably have to fill in a US Visa Application Form. This will ask you if you have ever been a member of the Communist Party.

1 Imagine that you are accusing someone in your class of a political crime.
a) Write the name of the person on a piece of paper, along with your accusation.
b) Give the paper to the investigator (your teacher).
c) The teacher reads out a list of accused people, with the crimes they are supposed to have committed.
d) You can then write new accusations about the named people.
e) The teacher collects these in.
f) The class can then hold a 'trial' of the accused, using this 'evidence'.
g) What does this activity suggest about the way McCarthy's campaign might have operated?

2 **a)** What two events caused many Americans to fear the spread of Communism?
b) How did Truman himself make the witch hunt worse?
c) Reply to the points in Source **B** from the point of view of an enemy of McCarthy.

d) What would the McCarron-Nixon Internal Security Act mean for Communists?
e) What argument did Senator Millard Tydings use against McCarthy?
f) How did McCarthy destroy Tydings' career?
g) Pick out points, words and phrases in Margaret Truman's biography of her father, President Truman, which suggest she may be one-sided in her views (Sources **D**, **E** and **G**).
h) How did some politicians further their own careers by supporting McCarthy? Name three politicians who did this.
i) What evidence is there on these pages to support the Tydings Report that McCarthy's claims were a 'fraud and a hoax on the American people' (Source **C**)?

3 What role did McCarthy play in the anti-Communist witch hunt?

Questions

America, 1945–60

▶ What was life like in America after the Second World War?

President Truman, 1945–53

Truman got Congress to pass a series of laws which became known as 'The GI Bill of Rights' (GI stands for 'Government Issue', the name given to American soldiers). These included an Employment Act to make sure that service men and women who had been in work before the war got the chance to have their old jobs back. They also got offers of cheap loans and free training at a college or university. This marked the beginning of huge growth in American education.

When Truman was elected for a second term as President in 1948, he brought in his 'Fair Deal' scheme.

- He increased the national minimum wage from 40 cents to 75 cents per hour.
- He got Congress to pass the National Housing Act in 1949 aimed at clearing slums in the inner cities and building nearly a million new 'housing units' by 1955.

President Eisenhower, 1953–60

In the 1952 presidential election Dwight Eisenhower was the Republican candidate. He had been a national hero since the Second World War but had never shown much interest in politics. 'Ike' won the election in a Republican landslide (Source **A**).

Eisenhower's lack of experience of politics was a big handicap. He had spent most of his life in the army.

- He did not enjoy political arguments and relied heavily on his advisers. Ike made few major changes.
- Eisenhower was President during one of the biggest economic booms in American history.
- He was easily re-elected in 1956.

Boom and strikes

After the Second World War, America's economy boomed. Large-scale strikes in many industries broke out in 1946 and 1947 as workers tried to get a bigger share of America's growing wealth.

- The most serious strikes were in the steel industry and at General Motors.

Source A President Dwight Eisenhower. What does the photo tell us about Ike's popularity?

- In 1947 Congress passed the Taft-Hartley Act which gave a 60-day 'cooling-off' period before any strike could take place.

The economy, population and education

The economy
- There was a worldwide demand for American goods.
- Between 1945 and 1967 the United States Gross National Product (the total value of all production) increased from $213 billion to $775 billion.
- By 1960 the United States was producing half of all the industrial goods in the world, even though Americans only made up 6 per cent of the world's total population.

Population
- In 1945 there were about 150 million people living in the United States.
- This had risen to over 200 million by 1968.
- The movement of people within the United States continued after the war. In the 1950s the population of California went up by 50 per cent, closely followed by Florida.

Education
- In 1945 there were over 600,000 people in universities and colleges. This had risen to 3.6 million by 1960.

The car and the suburb

The automobile became the symbol of America's wealth. Most American families had at least one car. This meant that people no longer had to live close to their place of work. Those who could afford it moved out of the city centres to the never-ending suburbs that were growing up around American cities (Source **B**). By 1960 over 20 per cent of American families lived in homes that had been built in the 1950s.

The classless society

In American suburbs the nearest shops, bars and clubs can be miles away, making the motor car more and more central to the American way of life. More and more people were able to afford a middle-class lifestyle, living in their own houses with 'mod-cons' such as televisions, washing machines and cars.

Poor America

However, not everyone shared in the growing wealth. As page 75 shows, millions of Americans continued to live in poverty. Many of these were black people. By the late 1950s unemployment was going up again and reached four million.

Source B Vast suburbs grew up around many American cities in the 1950s and '60s

1 a) List points to show why was there was an economic boom in America after the war.
b) Describe the main measures of the 'Fair Deal'.
c) Why was there a series of strikes in 1946–47?
d) What was the Taft-Hartley Act?
e) What kind of leader was Eisenhower?
f) What do we learn about the role of the car and the new suburbs from Source **B**?
g) What points might an American make in 1960 to support the claim that America was the best country in the world to live in?

2 In the 1950s the United States made regular 'Voice of America' radio broadcasts to the USSR and Eastern Europe, giving world news and news about life in America. Produce a script for a 'Voice of America' programme as though you are broadcasting in 1960, and make a tape of it.

Questions

President Kennedy, 1960–63

How successful was J. F. Kennedy as President?

John Kennedy, or 'Jack' as he was often called, was brilliant on television. In one of the closest elections ever, Jack beat the Republican candidate, Richard Nixon. At the age of 43, Jack was the youngest President in American history. The first Catholic President, he was clever, witty and good-looking, with a beautiful wife, Jacqueline. The Kennedys brought a new style and glamour to the Presidency. They seemed the perfect couple, a fairytale prince and princess.

Kennedy and change

The new President gave young men and women and blacks jobs in his government. Kennedy claimed that the United States was facing a 'New Frontier'.

The 'New Frontier' laws failed because many Republicans and some very conservative southern Democrats loathed Kennedy. Can you think why?

Source A   From the speech made by Jack Kennedy when he took office in January 1961

> The torch has passed to a new generation of Americans. We must bear the burden of a struggle against the common enemies of man: tyranny, poverty, disease and war itself . . . And so my fellow Americans: ask not what your country can do for you – ask instead what you can do for your country.

Kennedy's New Frontier

Civil rights
- Jack Kennedy backed the campaign by the blacks for civil rights.
- He hoped 'New Frontier' laws, like those of the 'New Deal', would improve the daily life of Americans, especially of the poor.
- Congress would have to pass the 'New Frontier' laws.
- Unfortunately Kennedy – unlike Roosevelt – was poor at handling Congress.
- In 1961 he asked Congress to support a Medical Help for the Aged Bill, which was aimed at starting national health insurance for old people. But Kennedy could not get the votes of enough Senators to support the bill.
- He tried to get an education law passed to allow the Federal Government to give more money to schools, especially in the run-down city areas. Again Congress threw out the bill.
- However, Kennedy did manage:
  - to increase social security
  - to get special training schemes set up for the unemployed
  - to start big new housing programmes.

Source B   The Kennedy family relaxing at home. What impression do you think the Kennedys wanted this photo to give?

Kennedy and crime

Meanwhile one of Jack Kennedy's brothers, Robert, started a crusade against organised crime, including the Mafia. Jack had made Robert Attorney-General in charge of the government's legal affairs.

Cuba

The Cuban crisis was Kennedy's biggest challenge. It made President Kennedy a national hero. Even his enemies admired how he had dealt with the affair. Abroad he was the champion of the West against Communism. In Berlin, he told a packed crowd: 'Ich bin ein Berliner!' (Source **C**). [I am a Berliner – unfortunately Kennedy's aides forgot to tell the President that a 'Berliner' in German is a kind of doughnut.]

Source C Kennedy speaks to the crowd in Berlin. How might a German have felt on hearing Kennedy's speech? What did he really mean by the words 'Ich bin ein Berliner'?

The Cuban crisis

- Communists gained control over Cuba in 1959.
- In 1961 many Cubans fled to America.
- Jack Kennedy backed Cuban exiles who invaded Cuba to try to overthrow its new Communist government.
- The army of Fidel Castro, the Cuban leader, easily beat the invaders at the place named 'The Bay of Pigs'.
- Castro turned to Russia for help against the Americans.
- In October 1962 a US spy plane discovered that the Russians were building nuclear missile sites on Cuba.
- Kennedy took firm action. He set up a naval blockade of the island and announced that the United States would sink ships entering the exclusion zone (the area within the blockade). This included Soviet ships sailing towards Cuba with missile parts.
- Kruschev, the Soviet leader, had to choose between backing down and removing the missiles or facing war with the United States. In the end he backed down.

Questions

You can split up these questions among the group or class, and have a round-table discussion on ideas and findings.

a) Put into your own words what Kennedy is saying in Source **A**.

b) What does this speech tell you about him?

c) What messages does Source **B** give you about the Kennedys? What instructions might they have given to the photographer about taking the picture?

d) What was the 'New Frontier'? How successful was it?

e) Why did Republicans loathe Jack Kennedy?

f) What success did Robert Kennedy have in his war on crime?

g) How might Americans have felt about Kennedy after the 'Bay of Pigs' affair?

h) What might their feelings towards him have been during and at the end of the Cuban Missile Crisis? Why might views have changed?

i) Give Source **C** a title and a new caption of about 30 words.

Death of a President

Who killed Kennedy?

The death of Kennedy

On 22 November 1963 John and Jackie visited Dallas in Texas. Source **A** shows them driving through cheering crowds with the Texan Governor John Connally and his wife.

Source A President Kennedy's motorcade in Dallas, shortly before the assassination

Source B
Willi Frischauer, Jackie Kennedy's biographer

There was a short, sharp sound but she thought it was a motorcycle back-firing. Suddenly Jack fell forward: 'My God,' he said, 'I'm hit!' She turned towards him and saw a questioning look in his eyes which she had seen often before. Then it dawned on her: 'Jack! Oh no! No!' she cried out. There was another cracking noise, no doubt about it this time, a shot which ripped into the President's skull.

Kennedy was dead. Within a few hours an ex-marine, Lee Harvey Oswald, was arrested and charged with the murder. Two days later Jack Ruby, a Dallas nightclub owner, shot Oswald dead. Did Oswald act alone? Or was there a plot? If so who organised it? The box on the next page looks at the evidence.

Who killed Kennedy?

Findings of the government's Warren Commission (24 September 1964)

1 'The Commission has found no evidence that anyone assisted Oswald in planning or carrying out the assassination.'
2 Abraham Zapruder's film (see Source **A**) shows that the second bullet, which hit the President in the back of the head, was fired from above and behind the motorcade.
3 Police found a recently fired rifle on the sixth floor of the Texas School Book Depository Building which the motorcade had just passed when the shots were fired (Source **C**).
4 Police had checked the Depository Building a few minutes earlier. They had seen Oswald on the second floor but this raised no suspicions.
5 Jack Ruby said that he had shot Oswald out of anger and a desire for revenge.
6 Oswald had been thrown out of the marines in disgrace.
7 Oswald's wife had told him that he was a weak man. Oswald's wife was Russian-born and Oswald himself had spent 18 months in the USSR.
8 Oswald had already tried to shoot General Edwin A. Walker.
9 Oswald had already shot dead a policeman before his arrest.

Findings of the Stokes Select Committee on Assassinations (June 1979)

1 'The scientific evidence suggested that it is likely that more than one person was involved in the President's murder. The Committee's investigation of Oswald and Ruby shows that they knew each other. Their relationship could have led to a plot. But the Committee admitted that it was unable to firmly identify the other gunman or the extent of the plot.' (*New York Times*, 3 June 1979)
2 Abraham Zapruder's film shows that the first bullet, which hit the President in the throat, could have been fired from in front of the motorcade.
3 Jackie Kennedy heard Governor Connally shout 'My God! They are going to kill us all'.
4 Oswald denied killing the President. Ruby could have shot him to silence him.
5 One of the police motorcyclists who was with the motorcade had accidentally left his microphone on. This recorded the assassination. It suggests the shots could have been fired from different weapons.

Source C
This photograph shows the book depository behind the President's car

John Kennedy's murder stunned the world. It was left to Lyndon Johnson, the new President, to get Congress to pass many of Kennedy's 'New Frontier' reforms. Page 75 looks at how Johnson started a 'War on Poverty' to improve the lives of millions of Americans.

Questions

1 **a)** What do Sources **A** and **C** suggest about how good a shot the killer(s) must have been?
b) Is there anything suspicious about the killing of Oswald?
c) The new President, Lyndon Johnson, set up the Warren Commission to look into the murder. It spent months finding out all it could. The Stokes Select Committee went over the same evidence with equal care.
- How do the two reports differ?
- What evidence is there that Oswald might have been acting for someone else?
- What motives might Jack Ruby have had for killing Oswald?
- What does Governor Connally's remark suggest?
- How important is the police microphone record of what happened?
- What does the Stokes Committee suggest might have happened?
- What evidence is there to support its view?

2 Was there a plot to kill the President? Or did Lee Harvey Oswald act alone? Use the evidence, and any other information you can find, to write your own report on the assassination.

3 Write a biography of Kennedy, using all the evidence you can find.

The Space Race

 ### Why did America put a man on the Moon in 1969?

Kennedy started the Apollo Moon Project. The Apollo Project was part of the 'Space Race' with the USSR.

Source A   By John F. Kennedy, May 1961

I believe that this nation should commit itself to achieving the goal, before this decade is out, of landing a man on the Moon and returning him safely to Earth.

I'm going to step off the ladder now. That's one small step for man, one giant leap for mankind.

Source B   By Neil Armstrong, the first man on the Moon

Source C
'Buzz' Aldrin stands on the Moon

The Space Race

- Ever since the Russians sent the first satellite, Sputnik 1, into space in 1957, Americans had feared that Soviet scientists were getting ahead of American scientists.
- In April 1961, shortly before the United States launched their first manned space flight, the USSR sent Yuri Gagarin into space in Vostok 1. This event stunned America. President Kennedy felt he had to prove that the United States was still the most advanced country in the world.
- In May 1961 Alan Shepard in Mercury 3 became the first American in space.
- In 1968 Apollo 8 was the first manned spacecraft to orbit the Moon.
- On 16 July 1969 Apollo 11 lifted off from Cape Kennedy in Florida.
- On 20 July the landing craft Eagle separated from the command craft, Columbia, and descended towards the Moon. If anything went wrong, the astronauts would die. A few hours later Neil Armstrong climbed down the ladder and on to the surface of the Moon, followed soon afterwards by 'Buzz' Aldrin (Sources **B** and **C**).

Thanks to television, millions of people around the world felt they were part of one of the biggest adventures in history. When the three astronauts returned to Earth they were world heroes.

Questions

1 a) Why was the Apollo Project started?
   b) What were the main worries as Eagle went down to land?
   c) What was the significance of Armstrong's message (Source **B**)?
   d) What does Source **C** tell us about the problems of sending a man to the Moon?

2 Some people were against the Apollo Project. They said that the billions of dollars it cost could have been better spent. Do you agree or disagree? Give reasons for your answer.

War on Poverty, 1963–68

How successful was the War on Poverty?

Just before he died, President Kennedy read a book about the way of life of poor people in America (Source **A**).

Large numbers of the poor lived in country areas such as the Appalachian Mountains. The poverty in the inner cities was the worst of all. Many of the poor lived in terrible housing (Source **B**).

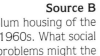

Source B
Slum housing of the 1960s. What social problems might the people in these houses have?

What should Kennedy do about these problems? The President died before he could act. In 1964 the new President, Lyndon Johnson, started his 'War on Poverty'.

Had Johnson done enough? The numbers of people living in poverty without enough food or adequate shelter fell from 22 per cent in 1959 to 11.6 per cent in 1975.

War on Poverty

- Johnson created an Office of Economic Opportunity and won the 1964 election on a campaign to provide new opportunities for the poor and unemployed.
- 'Job Corps' were set up, providing live-in camps for the jobless and for young people living in the inner cities.
- Neighbourhood Youth Corps provided training programmes for young people in many cities.
- Johnson started 'Operation Headstart' to provide extra funds to improve inner-city schools and to give pre-school education to many poor children. The aim of this was to try to change the attitudes of the young, to give them a sense of purpose and hope for the future.
- In 1966 Johnson finally got Congress to agree to a Medical Care for the Aged Act. This meant that people over 65 could get government aid for doctors' fees and hospital bills.
- The Social Security Act of 1966 increased federal help for the sick and disabled.

Questions

a) Draw up a table with two columns.
- In column 1 write down who were the 'other American' poor.
- In column 2 write down what their problems were.

b) As a class or small group, pool your findings. Produce a full list of problems.

c) Come up with a plan to solve each problem.

d) Compare your solutions with those of President Johnson. Which do you think would be most effective?

7 Civil rights

The beginnings

> **What was racial discrimination?**
> **What was the Civil Rights Movement?**
> **Why did it start?**

Freedom!

After the American Civil War, in 1865 black people in the American South were no longer slaves. But they had never gained equality with whites. Blacks had remained second-class citizens, with the worst-paid, unskilled jobs on farms and in factories. Their schools had far fewer books and bigger classes than schools for white children. In most southern towns and cities blacks were not allowed to use the same restaurants, parks, public toilets, transport and schools as whites. 'Separate' did not mean equal. White facilities were nearly always better. Black people found it hard to elect blacks into public offices such as town mayors to change things. Why was this?

Source A By Janet Harris, a civil rights worker for the National Association for the Advancement of Colored People

> A Negro in the Deep South who tried to register might lose his job or his credit. He might be beaten, have his house set on fire, or be killed. 'I don't want my job cut off,' one man explained. Another was more blunt: 'I don't want my throat cut,' he said.

The North

Things were not much better in the North. Although there were no 'Jim Crow laws' in northern states, black people usually had the worst-paid jobs and lived in the worst housing, often in inner-city slums such as Harlem. Since they lived in different areas blacks and whites usually went to different schools in the North as well as in the South.

The Second World War

The Second World War broke down some of the race barriers as blacks and whites had often fought side by side. In 1948 President Truman banned segregation (keeping blacks and whites apart) in the armed forces. Apart from that US governments did little to help blacks to be treated as equals.

Discrimination

The southern states had passed the 'Jim Crow laws' making the blacks 'separate but equal'.

- To vote in the United States you have to register. Southern states stopped blacks from registering in various ways.
- There were poll taxes on all those who registered. These stopped most blacks from doing so because they were too poor to pay the taxes.
- Literacy (reading and writing) tests – which were often rigged – stopped other blacks from registering.

If these steps did not work, whites took other steps to stop blacks from having the vote (Source **A**).

Civil rights campaign and Linda Brown

By the 1960s black American leaders headed a campaign for black equality. The campaign began in Topeka, Kansas in 1951.

Linda Brown, Topeka and integration

- The particular issue was whether a black girl, Linda Brown, could attend a local, all-white school.
- Linda had to walk over 20 blocks to get to her school in Topeka even though there was a local school just down the road.
- Linda's class was big, the classroom shabby and there were not enough books for each child (Source **B**). The all-white school just down the road was much better off.
- This was because the Topeka Board of Education spent much more money on the white school than on Linda's school for blacks.
- This angered Linda's father, Oliver Brown, so much that he took the Board of Education to court. He lost.
- With the help of the National Association for the Advancement of Colored People (NAACP), Oliver Brown appealed.
- In the end the case of *Brown* vs *Topeka Board of Education* reached the Supreme Court of the United States.
- On 19 May 1954 Chief Justice Earl Warren announced to a packed courtroom that the Constitution was 'colour blind' (Source **C**).
- The Supreme Court ordered the Topeka Board of Education to end segregation in its schools.

Non-violent protest

Martin Luther King called a protest meeting at his Dexter Avenue Baptist Church for the next evening. King believed in 'non-violent' protest. He got many of his ideas from the Indian leader Mahatma Gandhi who had led India to independence from the British by a peaceful campaign of not co-operating with the government.

The protest movement is born

Thousands of people turned up to the meeting that night. There was not enough room in the church, so loudspeakers were put up in the surrounding streets. Martin Luther King was the main speaker (Source **C**).

Source C   By Martin Luther King, on the bus boycott

There comes a time that people get tired. We are tired of being segregated and humiliated [put down], tired of being kicked about. We have no choice but to protest. We are protesting for the birth of justice. In our protest there will be no cross burnings. No white person will be taken from his home by a hooded Negro mob and brutally murdered. There will be no threats and bullying. Love must be our ideal. Love your enemies, bless them, and pray for them. Let no man pull you so low as to make you hate him.

The bus boycott

The meeting decided to start a boycott of Montgomery's buses (to refuse to ride on them).

In 1957 the Southern Christian Leadership Conference was set up and Martin Luther King became its President. From then on he devoted his life to the campaign for civil rights.

The bus boycott

- Leaflets were sent out all over Montgomery explaining what the boycott meant.
- On Monday 5 December 1955 hardly any blacks in the whole of Montgomery rode on the buses.
- The streets were filled with people walking to and from work and school. Children ran behind the buses shouting 'No riders today!'
- Blacks were normally the main users of the buses because few of them could afford cars. Now most of the buses went by empty or only half-full.
- The meeting in Montgomery decided they would only end the boycott when the bus company ended segregation.
- The churches of Montgomery started to run their own mini-bus service. Reporters from around the world came to Montgomery.
- Martin Luther King was suddenly famous and so was the cause of civil rights. People from many different countries gave money to keep the boycott going.
- Churches around the world gave their support.
- The bus company was in danger of going bankrupt.
- On 22 February 1956 Martin Luther King was arrested along with 100 others. He was charged with 'plotting an illegal boycott'. It was the first of many occasions on which King would be arrested. This time he was ordered to pay a $1,000 fine.
- A few white people now turned to violence. Bombs were planted in four black churches and by March, King's house had been bombed three times.
- The boycott continued. The protesters took their case to the courts.
- On 13 November 1956 the Supreme Court announced that segregation on buses was illegal.

Questions

1 **a)** Prepare a briefing leaflet for reporters from Britain in November 1956, explaining the bus boycott from the point of view of *either* a King supporter *or* the bus company.
   b) Explain why the bus boycott took place. Mention the roles of:
   - Rosa Parks (Source **A**)
   - Martin Luther King – as a speaker, and his ideas (Sources **B** and **C**)

   - peaceful protest
   - the bus boycott and its impact
   - the Supreme Court's decision.

2 **a)** What was the importance of the bus boycott?
   b) What role did Martin Luther King play in it?

Schools and colleges

**What was the struggle over desegregation about?
What shape did the struggle take?**

Source A Martin Luther King campaigning for black rights. What ide does the photograph give of King's rol

Desegregating schools

After the Supreme Court ruled against the Topeka Board of Education in 1954, many towns and cities began to 'desegregate' their schools. Often the most run-down black schools were simply closed down and the children were sent to the nearest white school.

● **Rioting in Clinton, Tennessee**
When the town of Clinton in Tennessee began to integrate its Central High School in 1956, riots broke out. Hundreds of whites stopped black students from entering the school. Within a few days this mob, including members of the Ku Klux Klan, had grown to over 3,000. They began to attack local black people. Many black people were so scared that they packed a few belongings and left town.

● **Conflict** Supporters of mixed schools (many of them white) felt they had had enough of this mob rule and decided to fight back using guns. Luckily the National Guard turned up to keep the peace and the leaders of the mob were arrested. Racists later blew up Clinton High School.

● **White Citizens' Councils** In the Deep South, White Citizens' Councils were formed to fight against the integration (mixing) of schools. They encouraged employers to sack blacks who stood up for their rights.

● **Congress** In Congress, Southern Senators signed the 'Southern Manifesto' in 1956, promising to campaign against integration by every means possible. (Senator Lyndon Johnson refused to sign it.)

Civil rights protest

In May 1957 the Southern Christian Leadership Conference organised a 'Pilgrimage of Freedom' to the Lincoln Memorial in Washington. Nearly 40,000 people took part. President Eisenhower held a meeting with civil rights leaders, including Martin Luther King, but little action was taken.

In 1957 King travelled 1,250,000 kilometres and made 208 speeches campaigning for black rights (Source **A**).

Little Rock, Arkansas

The town of Little Rock in Arkansas decided that it would integrate its schools a bit at a time.

● The Central High School would take in its first black student on 3 September 1957.

● The evening before, the Governor of Arkansas, Orville Faubus, announced that it would be impossible to keep law and order if black children started at the school.

● The next day, when nine black children, led by 15-year-old Elizabeth Eckford, arrived at the school, a large crowd of whites barred the way (Source **B**). Faubus had also sent Arkansas state troopers to make sure the children did not get in.

Source B Elizabeth Eckford remembers the day she was barred from school

I turned around. The crowd came towards me, yelling 'Lynch her! Lynch her!'

Source C US troops outside the Central High School in Little Rock, Arkansas. Why are the troops there?

The children were forced to go home. Black people in Little Rock took Faubus to court and he was ordered to remove the state troopers. President Eisenhower then sent 1,000 paratroopers to Little Rock to protect the black children on their way to school (Source **C**).

After the events at Little Rock, integration was speeded up in some towns. But by 1962 there had still been no integration at all in the Southern states of Alabama, South Carolina and Mississippi.

James Meredith

James Meredith, a southern black, was qualified to go to the University of Mississippi. The University offered him a place for September 1962. However, Ross Barnett, the Governor of Mississippi, said his officials would 'uphold the segregation laws of the State of Mississippi whatever the federal courts say'.

When James turned up to register at the University on 20 September he found the Governor himself barring the way (Source **D**). Day after day the Governor refused to let James Meredith in (Source **E**).

Source E By Janet Harris, a civil rights worker

President Kennedy made a series of phone calls to Barnett. [These failed. Kennedy placed Mississippi's National Guard under his command and sent in US Army troops.] . . . On 30 September Meredith was driven to the University in a convoy of army trucks. The Deputy Attorney-General went with him. There was a riot on the campus. The 320 federal marshalls who had been sent to the University were attacked by a mob of white students and townspeople. Flaming missiles, rocks, bricks, and acid were thrown at them. The marshalls fought back with tear gas. [The army won.]

James Meredith stayed on at the University. He went to all his classes with federal marshalls to protect him.

Source D Meredith being banned from the University of Mississippi. Describe what is happening in the photograph.

Opposition ends

It took the Civil Rights Act of 1964 to end segregation in the Deep South's schools and colleges. This law gave the President the power to hold back money from schools that did not make plans to integrate.

Questions

1 **a)** What happened at Clinton, Tennessee in 1956?
b) What do we learn from Source **B** about the attitudes of some whites to the civil rights protesters?
c) What does the text and Sources **C**, **D** and **E** tell us about the way some people tried to oppose the Civil Rights Movement?
d) Why is James Meredith famous?

2 Imagine you are a TV interviewer talking to James Meredith at the end of his first week at the University of Mississippi. Write an account of what he tells you about:

- his struggle to get to university
- what has happened to him in the past week
- his hopes and fears about the future.

3 **a)** Write titles and captions for the photographs in Sources **A**, **C** and **D** as a supporter of civil rights.
b) Compare your titles and captions with those of your partner.
c) What do they suggest to you about the use of photographs as historical evidence?

'I have a dream' – Martin Luther King

Why did Martin Luther King die?
What did he achieve?

William Moore was a white postman who had started a walk across the South to campaign for civil rights. His walk had been in the national news. A few hours after writing the entry in Source **A**, Moore's body lay by the road. Perhaps the Ku Klux Klan had shot him. Moore's death shocked Americans everywhere. Thousands of protesters continued the walk. When they reached the borders of Alabama many were arrested. Moore's killing was the latest in a series of more and more violent acts against black civil rights. Source **B** shows how a series of peaceful protests at bus stations ended in conflict.

The 'freedom rides'

In 1961 CORE (Congress of Racial Equality) started a series of 'freedom rides' on buses. Although the buses themselves had been de-segregated, the bus stations, shops and restaurants continued to have 'whites only' signs.

Source A   The last entry in the diary of William Moore

> 23 April 1963.
>
> Invited to chat with a few men who heard about my walk on television. They didn't think I'd finish my walk alive.

- Black civil rights protesters would catch buses to Southern bus stations and then try to use 'whites only' services. Sometimes they were beaten up.
- Robert Kennedy sent 500 US marshalls to protect a group of freedom riders who set off from Montgomery, but they were attacked. This sparked off a race riot.
- Finally Robert Kennedy got the Interstate Commerce Commission to end segregation in bus and rail stations and at airports.

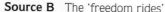

Source B   The 'freedom rides'

The Birmingham campaign

In 1963 Martin Luther King and other black leaders organised a new campaign against segregation in Birmingham, Alabama. Race relations here were among the worst in the South.

Birmingham, Alabama

- In April 1963 freedom marches began in Birmingham. At least 30,000 black Americans took part. Students and schoolchildren staged sit-ins and many people were arrested. Supporters (black and white) came from all over America to take part in the demonstrations.

- On Good Friday, King was arrested while leading a march through the centre of Birmingham.

- He was not allowed to contact anyone, not even his wife Coretta. She was so worried that she phoned Robert Kennedy.

- President Kennedy himself phoned the Birmingham Police Chief, Bull Connor, and a week later King was released.

- So many people were being arrested that the jails of Birmingham were full.

- On 3 May Bull Connor ordered his men to turn water cannon on a crowd of young protesters who refused to break up their march. The force of the water knocked down many of the young people, who then started throwing missiles at the police. Police dogs were set on the marchers and Connor jeered: 'Look at them run. Look at them niggers run!' (Source **C**).

- A week later the Ku Klux Klan held a big rally, lit crosses and made racist speeches. But the civil rights protests went on.

- President Kennedy demanded that the Birmingham Council should end segregation. A week after Connor had used his hoses and dogs, the Council gave in to the protesters' demands. It was the biggest victory so far in the civil rights campaign.

Source C
Black civil rights protesters are attacked by firemen using a water cannon. What might the people in the picture think of Connor, and why?

In June 1963 President Kennedy made a statement on television (Source **D**).

Source D From the public papers of J. F. Kennedy, 1963

If an American, because his skin is dark, cannot eat lunch in a restaurant open to the public; if he cannot send his children to the best school there is; if he cannot vote for the politicians who represent him; if he cannot enjoy the full and free life which all of us want, then who among us would be content to have the colour of his skin changed and stand in his place?

The Civil Rights Bill

Kennedy announced that he was asking Congress to pass a Civil Rights Bill that would make all forms of racial discrimination in public places illegal. Politicians such as George Wallace promised they would fight the Bill every inch of the way. Civil rights leaders believed that there was a real danger that Congress would not pass it. They organised one of the biggest demonstrations in American history.

On 20 August 1963 nearly 500,000 people marched into Washington (Source **E**), and gathered at the Lincoln Memorial. There, Martin Luther King gave his most famous speech of all (Source **F**).

Source F Martin Luther King's most famous speech of all

I have a dream that my four little children one day will live in a nation where they will not be judged by the colour of their skin . . . When we allow freedom to ring from every town and every hamlet, from every state and every city, we will be able to speed up that day when all of God's children, black and white, Jews and gentiles, Protestants and Catholics, will be able to join hands and sing in the words of the old Negro spiritual [song] 'Free at last! Free at last! Great God Almighty, we are free at last!'

Quoted in D. L. Lewis, *King: A Critical Biography*, Praeger Publishers, 1970

Source E Martin Luther King waves to demonstrators at the Lincoln Memorial, Washington on 20 August 1963. Why were the people in the crowd demonstrating?

In 1964 President Johnson finally got Congress to pass the Civil Rights Act.

Malcolm X

While Congressmen and Senators battled over the Civil Rights Bill there were more violent attacks on blacks. On 6 September 1963 a bomb went off during Sunday school in a Birmingham Baptist church. Four young black girls were killed. This kind of violence encouraged many blacks to believe that civil rights laws could not end discrimination against black people. This led to the growth of the 'Black Power' movement. The Black Power movement was strongest in the North. Its leader was called Malcolm X (Source **G**). He said that blacks should use a simple letter or number as their surname, because many of their names originated in the days of slavery, when black slaves were given their owner's name. Malcolm X and his supporters believed in using violence to smash white rule. He even wanted to set up his own black state.

Source G   Malcolm X. What messages does this photograph give about Malcolm X?

Voting Rights Act

In 1965, after further demonstrations centred in Selma, Alabama, Congress passed the Voting Rights Act. This gave the federal government power to take over the registration of voters in states where officials continued to try to bar blacks from voting.

Campaigning outside the South

Martin Luther King had decided that the non-violent civil rights campaign must be taken to the cities of the north and west as well. The headquarters of the Southern Christian Leadership Conference was moved to Chicago. Unemployment among northern blacks was twice as high as among whites. On average whites earned half as much again as blacks. Blacks usually lived in poor housing and often in black ghettos such as Harlem.

Rioting and murder

In 1964 there were major riots in Harlem, followed by riots in other northern inner-city areas. Things were made even worse when members of a rival Black Power movement shot Malcolm X dead.

War on poverty

Lyndon Johnson's 'War on Poverty' helped black Americans more than any other group. Despite this, the rallies, protests and riots continued. In 1967 there were four days of black riots in Newark, followed by riots in Detroit and other cities.

The killing of Martin Luther King

In 1968 the police violently broke up a demonstration of black strikers in Memphis, Tennessee. Later, Black Power demonstrators started a battle with the police in which a boy died.

Martin Luther King agreed to lead a peaceful march through Memphis, even though he had received many threats against his life. On the evening of 4 April 1968, King was standing on the balcony of a motel room in Memphis when a killer shot him dead.

As news of the murder spread across America (Source **I**) there were riots in the black areas of many cities. Over 30 people were killed and thousands injured.

Civil rights progress

By peaceful protest Martin Luther King had helped to change the attitudes of millions of white Americans towards blacks. When Governor George Wallace got ten million Southern votes in the 1968 presidential election, his was the last big campaign against desegregation.

In 1973 a black was elected as Mayor of Los Angeles, a city where only one person in eight is black. An opinion poll in January 1986 showed that 97 per cent of whites thought that blacks should have equal job opportunities with whites.

In January 1986 Andrew Young, the first black mayor of Atlanta, Georgia, pointed out that if it had not been for Martin Luther King there might have been a blood bath in parts of America in the 1960s.

Questions

1 a) Who was William Moore? What do we learn about him from Source **A**?
   b) How did 'freedom riders' help the civil rights campaign (Source **B**)?
   c) What in the panel on Birmingham, Alabama suggests that the city may have been close to major race riots in 1963?
   d) Why did Kennedy think that the civil rights protest in Birmingham was so important (Source **D**)?
   e) How might Connor's opposition have helped the civil rights movement?
   f) What did Martin Luther King hope to achieve (Sources **E** and **F**)?

2 a) What do you think of the views of Malcolm X?
   b) Under what circumstances (if any) would it have been right for American blacks to use violence to try to end segregation and racial prejudice in the United States?

3 a) What measures do you think the Civil Rights Act of 1964 should have contained?
   b) Draw up proposals of your own to help black people in America. How would you enforce your laws?

4 Design the front page of a newspaper for 5 April 1968. Include details of:
   • the shooting of Martin Luther King
   • King's contribution to the Civil Rights Movement
   • the effects that King's death is likely to have on race relations in the United States.

1990s race conflict

How far have the civil rights laws led to fair treatment for black Americans?
Could America be torn apart by race?

The Los Angeles riots

In 1992 the worst riots in American history took place in Los Angeles. The year before, a black driver, Rodney King, had been stopped by four white policemen for a minor motoring offence. A passer-by filmed them pulling Rodney King from his car and beating him up. A period of 81 seconds of the videotape showed the policemen hitting King 56 times with batons as he lay on the ground, and one officer kicked him in the head. King was left with twelve broken bones while the policemen laughed at what they had done.

In 1992, despite all the evidence, a court in Simi Valley in Los Angeles found the four officers 'not guilty' of assault. Ten of the twelve members of the jury were white. There were 10,000 known gun owners in Simi Valley. Within four hours of the verdict one gun shop alone had sold 500,000 bullets. Soon South Central Los Angeles was in flames (Source **A**).

Source A   By Josie Dew, a British tourist on a cycling holiday in Los Angeles at the time of the riots

The police lost control from the start and watched helplessly as swarms of people stormed the superstores and liquor stores, going on what the media called 'looting free-for-alls'. Hungry hands grabbed anything they could get. Whole families were swept along with the fiery flow and could be seen laughing and larking around as they casually loaded booty into their cars and pick-ups – televisions and videos, liquor and lamps, beds and rugs, suits and T-shirts and tools. It was a fun day out shopping with the kids, with the only requirement that the wallet be left at home.

It felt strange to be sitting in the suburbs watching television scenes of total anarchy that were taking placed just down the road – like watching Miami Vice and Thunderball and Terminator all rolled into one, only for real . . . Helicopters hovered over the burning city through growing clouds of thick, black, billowing smoke, filming the flames and the live rubber-burning car chases, the shell-shocked cops and the Korean community shoot-outs, the innocent truck drivers set upon by murderous gangs and beaten to head-smashed pulps . . . [After it was all over] everyone had something different to say. 'Revolution is the hope of the hopeless'; 'It's right to rebel'; . . . a hollow-eyed black man shuffled past me wearing a T-shirt with 'LOVE KNOWS NO COLOUR' across the front.

From Josie Dew, *Travels in a Strange State*, 1994

Source B   From the autobiography of US Vice-President Dan Quayle, *Standing Firm*, 1994

I was at the White House when the verdict in the Rodney King trial came down. Everyone was shocked at the acquittal, including the President [George Bush], since we had seen the videotape of the beating. But once the riots began in Los Angeles we were far more revolted by what we saw. The riots were a disgusting display of violence that achieved absolutely nothing.

President Bush had to send in federal troops to restore peace. By the time the riots were over rioters had started 5,383 separate fires, 55 people had been killed and 2,500 people had been seriously injured, including many fire fighters and police officers.

O. J. Simpson

In 1995, black American football star and TV personality O. J. Simpson went on trial accused of stabbing to death his ex-wife Nicole and her friend Ronald Coleman. The trial was watched live on TV by millions of people each day and became known as 'the trial of the century'. One poll after another showed that most white people believed Simpson to be guilty, and most black people were sure he was innocent.

Simpson was rich enough to have one of the best lawyers in the country, Johnnie Cochran. Cochran found evidence that one of the policemen who gave evidence against Simpson was a white racist who hated black people. Simpson's lawyer told the mainly black jury that it was really the LA police who were on trial (Source **C**).

Source C   By Johnnie Cochran, O. J. Simpson's defence lawyer

Race plays a part in everything in America and we need to understand that.

An audience of 180 million Americans watched on TV as the jury announced that O. J. Simpson was not guilty (Source **D**). That was more people than watched the first Moon landing. The O. J. Simpson trial divided Americans along race lines. Source **E** shows some important differences between black and white Americans in the 1990s.

In 1992 a Louis Harris opinion poll of 2,000 high school students showed that 30 per cent of American teenagers would be prepared to take part in racist attacks. Another 17 per cent said they would silently support such actions. The statistics in Source **E** highlight some of the differences between the US white and black populations.

Source D   O. J. Simpson on hearing the 'not guilty' verdict at the end of his trial

Source E   A divided nation: US race statistics

	White	Black
Population (1995)	216.1 million	32.9 million
Unemployment (1992)	6.5%	14.1%
Median family income* (1993)	$37,783	$21,548
In prison (1992)	0.16%	1.02%
Prisoners on 'Death Row' (1992)	1,464	1,018
Infant mortality** (1991)	7.7	17.1
'Illegitimate' births (1991)	20.2%	65.1%
With college education (1995)	59.8%	48.3%

*   One in three black Americans lived in households with incomes above $35,000 (£23,000) in 1995
** Numbers of infants who die before reaching the age of one per 1,000 live births

From the *Los Angeles Times*

The Million Man March

In 1994 Republicans took control of both houses of Congress. Despite President Clinton's protests they made big cuts in welfare spending and in programmes of 'Affirmative Action' which aimed at helping black people. On 16 October 1995 the Million Man March took place (Source **F**). British reporter Jonathan Freedland was there (Source **G**).

Source F   The Million Man March, 16 October 1995

For a day the city was theirs. From every corner of the United States they came, carpeting the National Mall all the way from the Washington Monument to the steps of the Capitol. No one was sure of the numbers but they looked like a promise fulfilled: a million black men.

Source G   From *The Guardian*, 17 October 1995

The march was organised by Louis Farrakhan, the leader of 'Nation of Islam'. Farrakhan spoke strongly against white people and Jewish people and called for a separate black state. The same day President Clinton spoke out against all forms of racism (Source **H**).

Source H   From *The Guardian*, 17 October 1995

White Americans and black Americans see the same world in very different ways. Whether we like it or not we are one nation. White Americans must acknowledge the roots of black pain. To our black citizens we must say your house too must be cleansed of racism.

Questions

1   **a)** What event sparked off the Los Angeles riots?
    b) Why do you think it only took one event to spark off such violent riots?
    c) Was Josie Dew an eye-witness to the Los Angeles riots (Source **A**)?
    d) How far do you agree with Vice-President Dan Quayle's view of the rioting (Source **B**)?

2   In what ways did the trial of O. J. Simpson divide America along race lines?

3   In pairs, imagine you are in an American high school on the day of the O. J. Simpson verdict. One of you takes the role of a black student and the other the role of a white student. Talk about how you see the racial divisions in America.

8 Political turmoil

America at war: Vietnam

▶ **What was the Vietnam War about?**
What impact did it have on America?

> If you are reading this letter you will never see me again because it will mean I am dead. The question is whether or not my death has been in vain. The answer is yes. The war that has taken my life and many thousands before me is immoral and unlawful. I had no choice as to my fate. It was decided by the war-mongering hypocrites in Washington.
>
> From Gloria Emerson, *Winners and Losers*, 1972

Source A By Keith Franklin, New York, 27 February 1970

Source **A** is from a letter Keith wrote to his parents just before he went to fight in Vietnam. They were only to open the letter if the nineteen-year-old Keith was killed. On 12 May 1970 he was dead, one of the 58,000 Americans who fell in Vietnam. What was the war about? What course did it take?

The Vietnam War

Vietnam had been a French colony. After the Second World War Communist guerrillas under Ho Chi Minh fought for Vietnamese independence.

- **1954** The Communists defeat the French. Vietnam is divided (Source **B**). North Vietnam becomes Communist.

- Communist guerrilla fighters called the Viet Cong, whom the North support, begin to control parts of South Vietnam.

- **1959** The Viet Cong rule over a third of the South.

- **1961** President Kennedy sends supplies and advisers to South Vietnam to try to defeat the Viet Cong.

- **1965** Lyndon Johnson announces 'Operation Rolling Thunder' – the full-scale bombing of North Vietnam.

- **1965** Johnson sends American combat troops to fight in Vietnam.

- **1967** Over half a million American soldiers are in Vietnam. Many went there under protest.

- **1968** The Tet Offensive
  • The Viet Cong attack most American positions in Vietnam, including the US Embassy in Saigon. There is fierce fighting, especially at Hue and Khe Sanh. Over 150,000 Vietnamese die, along with some 15,000 US troops. Two million Vietnamese are made homeless.

• There is mass American protest movement against the Vietnam War.
• Senator Robert Kennedy announces that he is campaigning to replace Johnson as the Democratic candidate in the 1968 presidential election. On 5 June 1968 Kennedy is shot dead.
• President Johnson says he will not run for President again.

- **1969** The Republican Richard Nixon takes office as President. He announces that he will 'Vietnamize' the War, which means withdrawing US troops and getting the South Vietnamese to continue the fight. Heavy bombing continues.

- **1970** Americans invade Cambodia to destroy Vietcong bases.

- **1970–73** Bitter fighting continues. Viet Cong control most of the countryside. Peace talks open (1972).

- **1973** A ceasefire is agreed. The last American combat troops are withdrawn from Vietnam. American Congress limits the powers of the American President to make war without the permission of Congress.

- **1975** North Vietnam launches a final attack and South Vietnam's government collapses. In April Saigon falls to the Communists.

Fighting in Vietnam

The American soldiers faced big problems. Most of the time the enemy guerrillas were nowhere to be seen. During the daytime they usually concealed themselves in the jungle or were hidden by friendly villagers. They attacked at night and then disappeared again. Many Vietnamese hated the American soldiers being in their country, especially when they saw their homes and villages destroyed in the fighting, or their families and friends killed.

Source B   Part of a letter written by a veteran, Richard H. Brummett, to the US Secretary of Defence Melvin Laird, on 27 October 1970

From July 1967 to July 1968 I served in the United States Army in Vietnam. My unit was involved in random shelling of villages with phosphorus shells, machine gunning of civilians, torture of prisoners, destroying of food and livestock of villagers and burnings of villages for no apparent reason. These are only a few of the many events that have been on my conscience . . .

Gloria Emerson, *Winners and Losers*, 1972

Source C   Vietnam in south-east Asia in March 1970. By this time Communist forces had taken over most of South Vietnam.

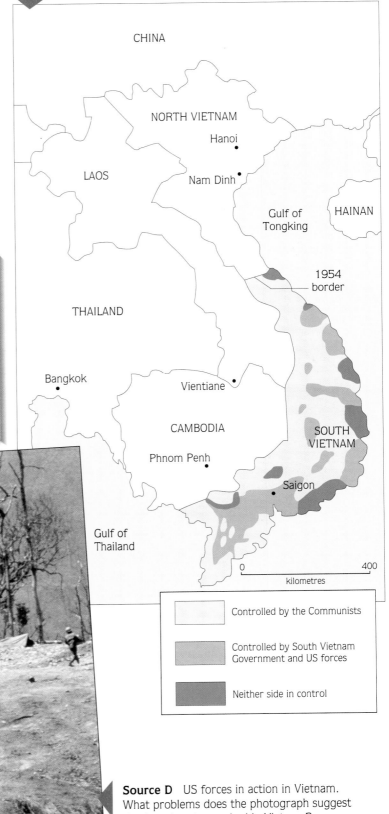

- CHINA
- NORTH VIETNAM
- Hanoi
- LAOS
- Nam Dinh
- Gulf of Tongking
- HAINAN
- 1954 border
- THAILAND
- Bangkok
- Vientiane
- CAMBODIA
- Phnom Penh
- SOUTH VIETNAM
- Saigon
- Gulf of Thailand

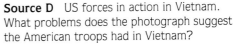

0   400
kilometres

Controlled by the Communists

Controlled by South Vietnam Government and US forces

Neither side in control

Source D   US forces in action in Vietnam. What problems does the photograph suggest the American troops had in Vietnam?

The impact of the war

By 1966 the US government was spending more on the Vietnam War than on the entire US welfare programme (Source **E**). The war cost $28 billion a year. Johnson claimed that victory would come soon. When no victory came, public distrust of the government grew.

The television war

Television brought the war into people's living rooms during the Tet Offensive. Night after night people saw for themselves the dead, wounded and dying American soldiers as well as Vietnamese people caught up in the fighting (Source **F**).

Source F   Part of a TV report on the Vietnam War by Walter Cronkite, the most respected television news presenter in America

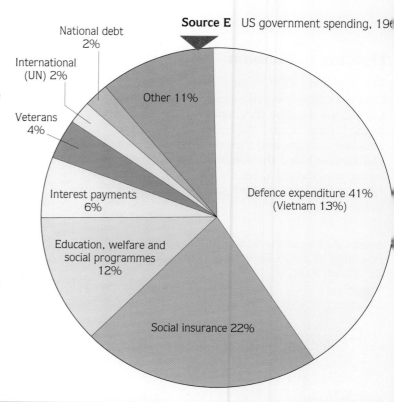

Source E   US government spending, 196[...]

- National debt 2%
- International (UN) 2%
- Veterans 4%
- Other 11%
- Interest payments 6%
- Defence expenditure 41% (Vietnam 13%)
- Education, welfare and social programmes 12%
- Social insurance 22%

Report from Vietnam. Khe Sanh was designed to be a small border stronghold. For reasons of US pride it has been built up into a major fortress where 55,000 marines are isolated. It is increasingly clear to this reporter that the only reasonable way out is to negotiate [discuss] not as victors but as a people of honour. A people who lived up to their pledge to defend democracy and did the best they could.

I would take time off work to go to anti-war demonstrations. It shocked some people who called me a Communist. The anti-war movement made a difference to everyone who took part. I think if there had not been such a movement they might have nuked Vietnam off the face of the earth [destroyed it with nuclear weapons]. It forced people to recognise what was going on or to become totally, unnaturally blind.

Source G   Quoted by Gloria Emerson in her book *Winners and Losers*, 1972

The protest movement

American public opinion began to turn against the war. TV programmes, newspaper and magazine articles and stories, poems and pop songs showed a growing hatred of the war.

Across America there were anti-war demonstrations. Students held sit-ins and sometimes rioted on their campuses. Millions of Americans could no longer understand what their country was fighting for (Source **G**).

Often the protests ended in violence. At Kent State University, National Guardsmen shot four students dead (Source **H**).

Source H A student at Kent State University shot dead. How would you feel if troops shot your friends dead while you were protesting about government policy?

In April 1971 Vietnam veterans held their own protest against the war (Source I).

Source I   By Gloria Emerson, reporter and historian

They started to come into Washington on a Friday – a strange looking army. All came with their discharge [from the army] papers so that people could not accuse them of being imposters, although some did anyway. There were a few men who did not have two legs and some who could not rise from wheelchairs. It did not matter that they were long-haired or bearded and their uniforms muddled. No one laughed at them or called out they were cowards and draft dodgers. There were times when they talked and sang and acted as if they knew what it was to be young . . . 'Son, I don't think what you are doing is good for the troops,' one elderly woman said to a man handing out leaflets. 'Lady, we are the troops,' he said.

From Gloria Emerson, *Winners and Losers*, 1972

As President Nixon withdrew troops from Vietnam, returning soldiers found there was no heroes' welcome for them. For those who survived in Vietnam the suffering goes on. Many Vietnam veterans find they cannot get the war out of their minds and often suffer from nervous illnesses. The vast cost of the war meant that welfare programmes such as the 'War on Poverty' never had a chance to be successful. The Vietnam War shook the belief in their country of millions of Americans.

Questions

1   Use the sources in this section to produce a case *either* for *or* against fighting in Vietnam. Use the following points to help you.

Source	Questions to consider
A	Was Keith's death in vain?
B	How did the soldier treat the Vietnamese people? How do you feel about his behaviour?
C	What does the division of the country suggest about support for the Viet Cong?
D	What problems did American soldiers face in fighting the Viet Cong?
E	What impact did the war have on the welfare programme?
F	What is Cronkite's advice? Why did he give it?
G	Why was the writer of this source demonstrating against the war?
H	What does this source tell us about the anti-Vietnam War movement?
I	Who were the men who were protesting? What do you think was the effect of the veterans' march on Washington? Why was the answer to the elderly woman devastating?
•	What does the panel on 'The Vietnam War' tell us about how America fought the war?

2   a) What part did television play in turning people against the war?
    b) What do we learn about the power of television from the evidence on these pages?

3   a) Research what it meant to fight in Vietnam.
    b) Take turns to role-play the part of a Vietnam veteran visiting your school (an American high school) in 1975.
    c) Ask questions about the war and discuss your views about it.

Watergate

Was Nixon guilty?

Source A From Bob Woodward and Carl Bernstein, *All the President's Men*, 1974

17 June 1972
9 o'clock Saturday morning

Early for the phone. Woodward fumbled for the receiver and snapped awake. The city editor of *The Washington Post* was on the line. Five men had been arrested earlier that morning in a burglary at Democratic headquarters [the Watergate building], carrying cameras and electronic gear. Could he come in? Woodward had worked for the *Post* for only nine months, but even so this didn't seem like a good assignment.

Source B President Richard Nixon. What kind of leader does the picture make Nixon appear to be?

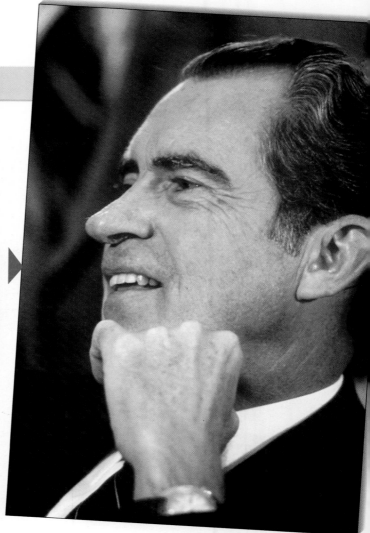

When Woodward arrived at the scene of the crime he started to ask questions:

1 Were the burglars working alone or were they acting on someone's orders?
2 What were the burglars after?
3 What were the burglars doing with cameras and electronic equipment?

The answers to these questions led to the greatest political scandal in American history.

Elected in 1968, President Nixon was a Republican. In 1972 he was running for a second term as President. Nixon easily defeated the Democratic candidate George McGovern in a landslide victory in November 1972 (Source **B**). Nixon's success as an international statesman played a big part. The President's close friend, John Mitchell, his ex-Attorney-General, ran CREEP – the Committee to Re-elect the President.

When the burglars went on trial early in 1973, some of Woodward's questions began to be answered. The burglars had acted on orders (Source **C**).

Source C From *The Washington Post*, a newspaper that had always been very critical of Nixon

FBI agents have proved that the Watergate bugging incident was part of a massive campaign of political spying and sabotage carried out on behalf of President Nixon's re-election. This aimed at smearing Democratic presidential candidates and disrupting their campaigns.

It also became clear that someone on Nixon's staff had tried to silence the burglars. Bernstein and Woodward were determined to find out who. Luckily, a senior member of Nixon's staff, 'Deep Throat', secretly told all. When in May 1973 the Senate Watergate Committee was set up it quickly became clear that all the men around President Nixon had been involved. H. R. Haldeman, Nixon's chief of staff, John Ehrlichman, Haldeman's number two, John Mitchell and John Dean, legal adviser to the President, all resigned.

Now a new question was being asked: how much did Nixon know (Source **D**)?

On 14 July 1973 Woodward received a phone call at home from a senior member of the Senate Committee. He said 'Congratulations. We interviewed Butterfield [an adviser to the President]. He told the whole story.' 'What whole story?' 'Nixon bugged himself.' The Senate Committee had discovered that Nixon had taped all his conversations in the White House Oval Office.

The Senate Committee demanded that Nixon hand over the tapes. At first Nixon refused. He denied he was involved in the Watergate affair even when advisers like John Dean confessed everything to the Senate Committee (Source **E**).

Source E By John Dean, addressing the Senate Committee

I began by telling the President that there was a cancer growing on the Presidency and it was important that it was removed immediately. I then proceeded to tell him that perjury [lying in court] had been committed and that for the cover-up to continue would require more perjury and more money.

When Nixon finally handed over the tapes, some were missing and others had had key passages rubbed out. He denied that he knew anything about this. Was Nixon lying? By June 1974, seventeen members of Nixon's government had been found guilty of various crimes. Congress began the process of dismissing Nixon from office. Source **F** was taken on 7 August 1974. On the next day Nixon resigned. Vice-President Gerald Ford became the new President.

Source D From Bob Woodward and Carl Bernstein, *All the President's Men*, 1974

Source F Richard Nixon and his family photographed during his resignation speech. How does the photograph suggest that Nixon wanted to be remembered?

1 Was Nixon guilty? You can carry out a classroom trial of Nixon, arguing for or against him.
   a) What view does Source **B** give of Nixon?
   b) What claims did *The Washington Post* make against White House officials early in 1973 (Source **C**)?
   c) What evidence is there that the accusation was accurate?
   d) If you were defending Nixon, how would you deal with Bernstein and Woodward's use of the evidence of 'Deep Throat'?
   e) What does the resignation of Nixon's staff suggest about Nixon's guilt or innocence?

   f) What do you think happened to the missing tape evidence?
   g) Does Dean's evidence suggest that Nixon was in charge of the 'cover-up'? If not, who might have been?
   h) What impression does Nixon want Source **F** to give of him?

2 Gerald Ford, the next President, pardoned Nixon. Why do you think he did so? Do you think he was right? What would you have done?

uestions

Index

Agricultural Adjustment Administration 43, 47, 51, 52
Apollo Moon Project   74
atom bomb   59, 63

Banking Act, 1933   43
Berlin Airlift   63
Birmingham, Alabama   83, 85
Black Power Movement   85
Bonus Marchers   40
bootlegging   22
Bush, President George   87

Capone, Al   24–26
Chaplin, Charles   12, 16, 17
Churchill, Winston S.   58, 59, 61
Civil Conservation Corps   43
Civil Rights (see race)
Civil Rights Bill   84, 85
Civil Works Administration   44
Clinton, President Bill   89
Cold War   60, 61, 62, 63, 74
Cooke, Alistair   4, 36, 42, 57
Coolidge, President Calvin   20, 30
Cuba   71

Depression, The Great   32–45
Dustbowl   46–49

Eighteenth Amendment   22
Einstein, Izzy   23
Eisenhower, President Dwight   65, 66, 68, 80

Fair Deal   68, 69
Fair Labour Standards Act   56
Farm Credit Administration   43, 47
farming   20, 33, 36, 37, 39, 43, 46–49
Farrakhan, Louis   89
Federal Emergency Relief Administration 43, 44
film industry (see Hollywood)
First World War   6–7, 30, 39, 40
Fitzgerald, F. Scott   14
flappers   13
Four Freedoms   58
Ford, Henry   18, 19
Fordney-McCumber Tariff Act   30, 33
freedom rides   82

gangsters   24–26
Great Crash   32–39

Harding, President Warren   11, 20, 30
Hiroshima   59
Hitler, Adolf   52, 58
Hollywood   12, 15, 16, 17
Hoover, President Henry   38, 39, 40
Hoovervilles   38, 39, 49
Hopkins, Harry   44, 45

immigration   8–9, 31

industry   7, 8, 9, 10, 12, 18, 19, 20, 21, 32–45, 51, 54, 55, 56, 59, 62ff, 68
Iron Curtain   61
isolation   11, 58, 60

Jazz Age   12, 13, 14
Jim Crow laws   76
Johnson, President Lyndon   73, 75, 80, 84, 85, 90, 92

Kellogg-Briand Pact   31
Kennedy, Joseph   15
Kennedy, Mrs Jacqueline   70, 72
Kennedy, President John F.   70–73, 74, 75, 81, 83, 84, 90
Kennedy, Senator Robert   71, 82, 90
Keynes, John Maynard   55
King, Martin Luther   78, 79, 80, 82, 83, 84, 85, 86, 87
Korean War   65, 67
Ku Klux Klan   14, 27–29, 80, 82, 83

League of Nations   11
Lend–Lease   58
Lindbergh, Charles   12, 13
Little Rock   80
Long, Huey   50
Los Angeles Riots 1992   87
Lusitania   6

Malcolm X   85
Marshall, Secretary of State, George   62, 63, 65
Marshall Plan   62, 63
McCarthy, Joseph   64–67
McCarthyism   64–67
Meredith, James   81
Model T. Ford   18, 19
Montgomery Bus Boycott   78

National Association for the Advancement of Colored People (NAACP)   76, 77, 78
National Industrial Recovery Act   43, 52
National Recovery Administration   44
New Deal   40–55
New Frontier   70, 73
Nixon, President Richard   64, 70, 90, 93, 94–95
North Atlantic Treaty Organisation (NATO) 63

Oswald, Lee Harvey   72, 73

Pearl Harbor   59
Pickford, Mary   16
Prohibition   22–26
Public Works Administration   44, 45

race   8, 9, 10, 27–29, 76–90
railroads   8, 9
Reagan, President Ronald   53
Red Scare (see also McCarthyism)   31

Resettlement Administration   47
Roosevelt, Eleanor   52
Roosevelt, President Franklin D.   23, 40, 41, 42, 43, 44, 45, 46, 47, 50, 51, 52, 53, 54, 55, 56, 57, 58, 59, 60
Russia (see USSR)

Sacco and Vanzetti   31
Second World War   58–59
Sedition Act 1918   7
Simpson, O. J.   88, 89
slavery   9, 76, 85
Southern Christian Leadership Conference 79, 80, 85
Space Race   74
speakeasies   22ff
Stalin, Joseph   52, 59, 60, 61, 63
Statue of Liberty   8
Steinbeck, John   46, 47, 48, 49
Stephenson, D. C   29
Stokes Select Committee   73
strikes   9, 10, 20, 21, 55, 56, 68
St Valentine's Day Massacre   26
Supreme Court   5, 21, 52, 76
Swanson, Gloria   15

Teapot Dome Scandal   30
Tennessee Valley Authority   47, 50
Tet Offensive   90, 92
Thompson, Mayor Bill   25
Topeka Board of Education   76, 77, 80
Torrio, John   24
Truman Doctrine   62
Truman, President Harry S.   59, 61, 64, 65, 66, 68, 76
trusts   10
Tydings, Senator Millard   65, 67

Un-American Activities Committee   66
unemployment   32, 35–41ff, 46, 48, 49, 51, 54, 55, 58, 59, 68, 69, 75, 85, 88
Union of Soviet Socialist Republics (USSR) 31, 51, 58, 59, 60, 61, 62, 63, 64, 65, 67, 71, 74
United Nations   60

Valentino, Rudolph   15, 16
Versailles Treaty   11
Vietnam War   90–94
Volstead Act   22

Wall Street Crash   32–35
War on Poverty   75, 85, 93
Warren, Chief Justice Earl   77
Warren Commission   73
Watergate   94–95
Wilson, President Woodrow   6, 7, 10, 11, 30
Women's Christian Temperance Union   22
Works Progress Administration   45, 57

Yalta Conference   60